BEAT
THE
BOOZE

Edmund Tirbutt, a multi-award-winning journalist and health insurance consultant, has been teetotal for over 24 years after overcoming a serious drink problem. **Helen Tirbutt**, a communications and change management consultant, has been teetotal for five years after giving up alcohol for lifestyle reasons.

Prior to writing either this book or their previous market-leading title *Beat the Booze*, the authors knew numerous people with drink problems. Some they managed to help, others they didn't. If they'd had the knowledge in those days that they have now, they feel the outcomes for those they couldn't help may have been very different. These life experiences have given them a passionate desire to help other problem drinkers and their friends, families and work colleagues.

HELP THEM
BEAT
THE
BOOZE

How to survive life with a problem drinker

Edmund Tirbutt & Helen Tirbutt

RODALE

This edition first published 2011 by Rodale
an imprint of Pan Macmillan, a division of Macmillan Publishers Limited
Pan Macmillan, 20 New Wharf Road, London N1 9RR
Basingstoke and Oxford
Associated companies throughout the world
www.panmacmillan.com

ISBN 978-1-9057-4479-4

Book design by e-type, Liverpool

Printed in the UK by CPI Mackays, Chatham, ME5 8TD

This book is intended as a reference volume only, not as a medical manual. The
information given here is designed to help you make informed decisions about
your health. It is not intended as a substitute for any treatment that you may
have been prescribed by your doctor. If you suspect you have a medical
problem, we urge you to seek competent medical help.

Mention of specific companies, organizations or authorities in this book does
not imply endorsement of the publisher, nor does mention of specific companies,
organizations or authorities in the book imply that they endorse the book.
Addresses, websites and telephone numbers given in this book were correct at
the time of going to press.

Visit **www.panmacmillan.com** to read more about all our books and to buy
them. You will also find features, author interviews and news of any author
events, and you can sign up for e-newsletters so that you're always first to hear
about our new releases.

LIVE YOUR WHOLE LIFE™

We inspire and enable people to improve their lives and the world around them

Contents

Acknowledgements

We would like to express our immense gratitude to all the experts, case studies, authors, publishers and other individuals and organizations who have played a part in helping us to produce this very worthwhile book.

Introduction

Anyone whose life significantly overlaps with that of someone who has developed a drink dependency is likely to feel they have been dealt a pretty rough hand. If you are the partner, friend or colleague of someone with a drink problem then you have no doubt been through a great deal of pain and heartache already, and you may even be at your wits' end. Life with someone who has a problem with alcohol can be exhausting and all-consuming. What is more, if you continue to try and help that person for any length of time you may end up being as compulsive and ill as the person you have been trying to help – a situation commonly described as being 'co-dependent'.

You may think you are skilfully acting as some form of amateur therapist by providing support and a friendly ear but, because you are constantly taking the side of the addict in your life, you are actually making things much worse for them. This may sound harsh, but if we don't bring the matter to your attention things will, unfortunately, only get worse.

However, the good news is that there are plenty of practical steps that anyone who knows or lives with a problem drinker can take to reduce or alleviate the pain and suffering experienced both by the drinker and by themselves. So if you are in a really desperate and lonely place right now because of someone else's addiction problem, we urge you to read on.

We have known several people who have died as a direct result of alcohol abuse and, because we were unable to find an easy-to-read guide that detailed how friends and loved ones could cope with such an individual, we felt largely powerless to help. Looking back, however, we believe that if we'd had access to the practical information contained in *Help Them Beat the Booze* the outcomes to these cases could have been very different and we could have spared ourselves a great deal of unhappiness.

In particular, we are very proud to refer to some exciting new modern methods of treating alcohol addiction in this book, many of which you've probably never heard of before. These have demonstrated spectacular results and may be worth trying if other more traditional methods, such as self-help groups, rehabilitation clinics and addiction counselling, have not proved to be as successful as you'd hoped.

If a drinker suffers from chronic anxiety, for example, the solution may be to introduce them to the Ameisen Baclofen Programme in conjunction with their GP. This has been extremely effective in removing the cravings for alcohol, and we have seen the lives of individuals we have introduced to this approach improve beyond recognition, even when spells in rehab and attendance at AA had previously failed.

As no two drink problems are identical, we make extensive use of detailed case studies to illustrate a range of different real-life scenarios. Although in some cases names and details of the characters involved have been changed to disguise their identities, these are real people detailing genuine accounts of the issues they have had to face. Some of these are moving, some encouraging, some inspiring, but it is our hope that in reading them you'll be able to identify with much of the trauma described and learn both from the techniques these individuals have successfully tried and the mistakes that, in retrospect, they realize they made.

These case studies, and the advice in this book as a whole, offer a wealth of information on how anyone affected by other people's alcohol abuse can help themselves. The fact that you are reading this book at all is an important first step. It's time for you to focus on your own happiness and wellbeing and realize that you have nothing to feel guilty about. By doing that you'll not only be helping yourself, ultimately you will also be helping the drinker whose life or workplace you share.

Edmund and Helen Tirbutt

CHAPTER ONE

Time to Take a Deep Breath

I f someone you love is drinking heavily and dangerously, you may feel like a pilot who has lost control of their plane. As you hurtle forwards, it can seem as though there are no more levers left to pull and no options remaining on the dashboard. You may find yourself feeling permanently angry, abused and used and it can be very difficult to talk to anyone about what you're going through. Furthermore, often when you do manage to talk to someone, you get strangely contradictory advice.

It's time to take a deep breath and apply the brakes. Help has arrived. We have had first-hand experience of life with problem drinkers, and this made us determined to produce a useful and easy-to-understand resource to help the partners, families, friends and colleagues of those with drink problems.

We have read other published material on the subject of alcohol abuse and interviewed numerous leading alcohol experts, friends and loved ones of those with drink problems as well as many problem drinkers, and the fact that one of us used to have a serious drink problem has provided further valuable insight. It is our aim to provide you with some useful strategies so you can help yourself, help the drinker in your life and start to address the problem.

It is worth saying at this point that even if the drinker is an acquaintance or work colleague you are not especially close to, you may still be able to help them. Simply passing on contact details for appropriate sources of help could prove a life saver, even if they don't pay any attention to it for several months or years. Furthermore, if the drinker's condition is not yet too serious and they are interested in cutting down rather than giving up, you may be able to play a pivotal role (see Chapter 3).

Before we get started, the first point we would like to make is that you are not alone, despite how you may be feeling. According to the World Health Organization, about 76 million people worldwide suffer from alcohol-related disorders at any one time. And because each problem drinker affects many other people, there are hundreds of millions of people worldwide in a similar position to yourself. So take a deep breath and read on.

Time to Stop the Guilt

If the person you are trying to help is a close family member, it is absolutely crucial that you stop blaming yourself for your loved one's condition. It is not your fault. You didn't cause the problem, even though the drinker will doubtless have regularly tried to blame you for doing just that. Nothing you could say or do will actually make someone drink. Even if your behaviour has caused them to be stressed and anxious, the fact that they choose to react to the situation by turning to alcohol is their choice and their choice alone – whatever the circumstances that have contributed. Not everyone chooses to use alcohol as a coping mechanism when they have problems.

'The alcoholic is an expert at projecting his own guilt feelings onto you. You become an expert at accepting them. When he avoids responsibility for his behaviour, yelling, "You drive me to drink!" you take it on yourself.

'You begin to think that if you were a better wife, he would not drink. He agrees. The children start to think that if they were better kids, he would not drink. He agrees with them, too. You tread carefully in order not to set off your alcoholic. Of course, this does not work either.'

Janet Geringer Woititz from Marriage on the Rocks

Just because you didn't cause someone's drink problem doesn't mean that you are powerless to help them do anything about recovering from it, or indeed powerless to help yourself recover from the detrimental impact that your relationship with the drinker has had on your life. There are many steps you can take to overcome co-dependency.

Finding an Approach That Works

The extent to which you will be able to help a drinker will depend very much on the particular circumstances of your individual case. What stage, for example, is the drinker at in their 'drinking career'? There can be a huge difference between someone who has been abusing alcohol for five years and someone who has been doing so for thirty years. What is your relationship with the drinker? Trying to help someone you live with can involve very different considerations from trying to help a sibling or parent who lives on their own hundreds of miles away. And perhaps most importantly of all, is the drinker still in denial, or are they trying to help themselves and willing to discuss the issue with you?

You may have read books or received advice from friends or medical professionals to the effect that there is nothing you can do to help a problem drinker, and that the only way they will recover is when they hit their own 'rock bottom'. This may or may not turn out to be the case in your particular situation, but we feel it represents an unduly defeatist attitude as a starting point.

There are certainly a number of approaches you can try which have been used with success to help the drinker come to the conclusion that they need to seek professional help. There are also a number of potential cures available that neither you, nor the drinker, nor those from whom you have previously sought advice, may have heard of. Some approaches and forms of treatment may work for the drinker in your life, while others may not, because each case is different and you will need to find the solution most suited to your situation. In some ways you will need to adopt a system of trial and error, but don't panic, we will talk you through each approach, so that you can work out what might be effective for you and the drinker you're trying to help.

The 'Key' Finding

Professor Cary Cooper, who is Professor of Organizational Psychology and Health at Lancaster University Management School, likens the task to having a bunch of keys and not knowing which one fits the door. You may have to try key after key.

He says, 'I believe you should never give up trying to get them to seek help, although you may at times have to stop being proactive and simply leave the key in the lock without trying to turn it. Leave it to them, but let them know you care about them and that you will listen, and maybe they will come to their own conclusions. They need a soul mate, someone who is not patronizing or judgemental, so, even if you've tried several times to get them to seek help, just be there.'

If you are reduced to leaving the key in the door without turning it, you should still be taking an active interest in your own welfare. Indeed, your co-dependency could have made you almost as ill as the drinker and, as we shall explain, there are steps you can and should take to help yourself.

If the drinker is your partner or spouse, then helping yourself could necessitate moving out of the family home or getting divorced in order to distance yourself from the problem. But this does not necessarily mean switching off the life support machine.

*

However slim the chances of recovery, while there is life there is hope and, if you make it clear that you are prepared to resume contact if the drinker eventually chooses to go dry, this can in some cases make the difference between life and death.

As you will see from the case study of Dorothy Sawyer at the end of this chapter, just being prepared to receive letters from a former partner whilst they are in a rehab clinic could make all the difference to them, but it does not have to be a source of serious inconvenience to you, even if you have subsequently started another relationship.

Please don't think we are saying that you don't have the right to decide when enough is enough. You most certainly do, and this may well end up being the only course of action open to you. Indeed, detaching yourself from the drinker and getting on with your life in a way that allows you to be fulfilled could even act as a valuable lifeline to the drinker by making them realize that they need to help themselves. It will also clearly benefit you. Just bear in mind that there is a difference between detaching yourself from and totally disowning someone, and between continuing to take responsibility for someone and continuing merely to take a passive interest in them.

> 'Detaching does not mean we don't care. It means we learn to love, care, and be involved without going crazy. We stop creating all this chaos in our minds and environments. When we are not anxiously and compulsively thrashing about, we become able to make good decisions about how to love people, and how to solve our problems. We become free to care and to love in ways that help others and don't hurt ourselves.'
>
> Melody Beattie from *Codependent No More*

Some alcohol experts will tell you that there are instances of people whose drink problems have become so severe they simply don't want to live, and that there is nothing you or anybody else can do to help them. In effect, they are using alcohol to commit suicide in a long-drawn-out fashion.

These experts are certainly not wrong. After all, there must be people out there who have done things that are so utterly unconscionable they would never discuss them with anyone, however much counselling they were offered. What, for example, happens to all those hit-and-run drivers who never get caught? Would they be able to live with their guilt, or would some of them turn to drink?

Never Say Never

Nevertheless, we would argue that there will never be any way of telling with absolute certainty whether someone is beyond help until they are actually dead and, just as people make remarkable recoveries from conditions like cancer after being told they have only months to live by the medical professionals, so there are cases of drinkers who have managed to go dry after virtually everyone has written them off.

As tough as this may sound, you might have imagined attending the funeral of someone you know with a drink problem. Indeed, when it seemed like they weren't going to survive a period of slipping off the wagon you may even have secretly wished they would die because it would make life so much easier for you and everyone else around them. There's no need to feel guilty if you've experienced such thoughts because they are extremely common amongst people in your situation. It isn't easy. We know, we've been there.

You may also have experienced the almost indescribable feeling of elation that occurs if a drinker you know manages to pull through a setback and once again provide cause for renewed hope. What you thought was going to be the end proved once again to be no more than a temporary relapse.

Dr Alex Wodak, Director of the Alcohol and Drug Service at St Vincent's Hospital in Sydney, says, 'Alcohol dependence is a treatable condition. Results of treatment are similar to the results seen when doctors treat other chronic conditions. Like many of these other conditions, relapse is part of the clinical picture. Results of treatment in the short term are often disappointing, but gratifying results are often seen in the long term.'

Who is to say that the next period of recovery won't be the one that finally proves sustainable? How do you know that the drinker won't finally go to the lock and turn the key themselves, or that you won't eventually stumble across a different key that finally does the trick?

There are, in fact, a number of significant new potential treatments that have recently become available, but which you are unlikely to hear about from the average GP. Similarly, your drinker is unlikely to hear about them from attending AA or other conventional self-help groups. We pay attention to all these developments because we know they have changed the lives of many people for the better and we're determined to help them change the lives of many more.

Be Open-minded

We've devoted the whole of Chapter 6 to considering some of the newer treatments for combating alcohol addiction, such as the Ameisen Baclofen Programme, the Sinclair Method and a nutritional approach known as The 101 Program. You might consider these if traditional methods such as medications, residential rehabilitation, counselling with addiction therapists and self-help groups have so far failed.

'Some people are able to halt their compulsive behaviour with the help of twelve-step programs like AA and commonly prescribed medications like Campral, Antabuse and Revia. But for the vast majority of people with addiction, these are not enough. They weren't for me. Which is not to say that AA didn't help…until I found an effective medication in baclofen.'

Dr Olivier Ameisen from The End of My Addiction

It is our considered opinion that any significant improvement in the treatment of alcohol addiction will result from new medical advances because they tend to be less resource intensive than the traditional approaches and show the potential for producing consistently higher success rates.

If an approach like the Ameisen Baclofen Programme fulfils the potential that it has demonstrated at the time of writing it could completely revolutionize the treatment of alcohol addiction worldwide. One of our key messages to you in your quest to find a solution to your loved one's problem is for you always to keep an open mind.

One of the few criticisms we would ever wish to make about those who work in any area of combating alcohol addiction is that they tend to be blinkered towards the particular approach they use and can be incapable of recognizing any merit in alternative methods. Likewise, one quality we have noticed that distinguishes most of the top addiction experts from lesser lights in the field is that they are willing to consider virtually anything that could be effective – even if it doesn't necessarily suit their own commercial agenda.

Dr Niall Campbell, Consultant Psychiatrist at The Priory Hospital, says, 'I would never rule out the newer treatments, and I follow them with interest, but a lot needs to be found out about them before we have confidence they will work. Because drinkers are so different, if professionals lump everything together and say one size fits all it just will not work.'

We have virtually nothing but praise for AA and for the 12 Step approach as a whole – a version of which is used by most rehabilitation clinics – as they have made a huge difference to millions of people's lives and may well constitute the most appropriate starting point for attempting to overcome alcohol addiction in a great many cases. Nevertheless, the 12 Step approach has changed little in the seventy-five years it has been in existence and, just because it clearly can prove effective, doesn't mean that other more modern methods can't work as well.

Although the fact has never been terribly well publicized, Bill Wilson, co-founder of AA, at one time tried to introduce nutritional methods into the AA experience, but his efforts were rejected by the membership.

'Since I first started working closely with Bill Wilson, co-founder of AA, I have believed that a person who is actually well will not become addicted to alcohol...The physicians of AA not only refused to respond to the promising results of our research, but also dismissed Bill Wilson's efforts to introduce nutritional treatment methods into the AA experience.'

Dr Abram Hoffer, in his foreword to *Alcoholism: the Cause & the Cure* by Genita Petralli

Professor Keith Humphreys, Professor of Psychiatry at Stanford University in California, USA, says, 'I agree with anything that works. It's an interesting phenomenon that the followers are sometimes more dogmatic than the prophets. Bill Wilson had nothing against medications and said it would be wonderful if there were a medicine for alcoholics.'

Involve a Third Party

Another vital message we would like you to grasp right from the outset is that, however good your intentions, the fact that you have longstanding feelings for someone with a drink problem and have an existing relationship with them will make it very hard for you to see the wood for the trees.

Jeffrey Huttman PhD, Licensed Clinical Psychologist and Chief

Clinical Officer at Challenges, a private addictions and mental health treatment centre based in Florida, USA, says, 'Family members wishing to be supportive of a loved one's abstinence are often faced with a difficult task because they are not usually in the best position to provide objective advice or recommendations due to their close relationship with the individual who is struggling.'

We cannot therefore stress strongly enough the importance of involving a third party. This could be your GP, a therapist or counsellor or someone involved in social care. Ideally they should have relevant professional experience so that they can bring valuable expertise to the recovery process, but even if they don't they will at least be able to provide the drinker with the reassurance that there is someone else to help, to take an objective viewpoint and to safeguard against denial by making sure that alcohol doesn't continue to be the elephant in the room.

A third party is also likely to enjoy a consistently higher standard of communication with a drinker than a friend or loved one, because the drinker is less likely to take the advice they offer as personal criticism. When someone takes criticism personally from someone they know they tend to answer back and pick out all their faults, but with a third party, even if they wanted to answer back, they wouldn't be able to because they wouldn't know their faults.

For this reason we have known drinkers who have found that a family member they aren't very close too, such as a sister they didn't see much of or get on with when they were younger, can act as a useful, objective third party.

Dr Francis Keaney, Consultant Addiction Psychiatrist at the National Addiction Centre, which is part of the Institute of Psychiatry at King's College, London, says, 'If you are involved with someone at whatever level with an alcohol problem, the first message is that someone outside "the system" who doesn't know you needs to be involved. Until that happens, family members or work colleagues are torturing and driving themselves insane inside "the system".'

As well as helping the drinker, the presence of an objective third party can act as an invaluable sounding board for you to determine what course of action you should take when dealing with the drinker. Some of the decisions you'll be faced with can be very finely balanced and should only be taken after the potential benefits and risks have been weighed up carefully.

A classic example of the type of dilemma you could find yourself in is when you become aware of the futility of continually giving the drinker money when they ask for it. Deep down you may be certain that the best course of action would be to stand your ground and refuse the request as it's been made once too often. Quite apart from the fact that you may not be able to afford to give them more money, you're also not acting in the drinker's best interests by 'enabling' them – giving them cash is, after all, funding their addiction habit.

At the same time, you may be concerned that not handing over more money could result in you losing the drinker's love or friendship. More worryingly still, you might fear for what could happen to the drinker; they could, for example, try to take their own life or turn to crime in order to raise the funds they require. Whatever you decide (or do not decide), this is a stressful situation to deal with.

'Experience shows that when people love someone, they give him the benefit of the doubt, again and again. They keep trying in hope the individual will finally "see the light" and change. This would be a great strategy except for one problem. Most people try the *same* tactics over and over. The sad thing is they do this not because what they are doing works but because it is the only way they know how. If you think about it, you can see it makes no sense.'

Robert J. Meyers and Brenda L. Wolfe from
Get Your Loved One Sober

Similarly, if a family member with a drink problem lives on their own in a different part of the country, should you continue to drop everything and drive over there whenever they fall off the wagon or need help? If you continue to do so, you are enabling the drinker in the sense that they are far more likely to relapse if they know they are going to be rescued.

If you are not on hand to drive the drinker to their GP to undergo a medical detox and to spend several days with them during the detox process then your loved one might die. They might, on the other hand, pull through against the odds, and the near-death experience may prove to be the 'rock bottom' they needed to reach to manage a sustained recovery. But can you afford to take the risk?

Every family or situation is unique and there is no one universally right answer, so it is important that any counsellor or practitioner working with you goes through your particular circumstances, looking at the advantages and disadvantages of particular approaches. Addiction counsellors and GPs can do this and, even if they cannot actually make the final decision on your behalf, you may benefit simply from the assurance of knowing you are not alone in facing these dilemmas. Support is vital.

Get Out and About

An additional key message is one that should benefit both yourself and the drinker, and it is: get out and meet as many people in similar situations to yourself as possible. Joining a local Alcoholics Anonymous group or other similar self-help group is an essential starting point and, if your loved one is in, or has been in, a rehab clinic, make sure you take advantage of the opportunities most of these organizations provide for the families and friends of those they are treating.

'Anyone who has experienced the devastating effects of another's alcoholism is welcome to Al-Anon. Even if we feel we were only mildly affected, we belong. Here we come to know that laughing together in spite of the darkness and pain we experienced is one of Al-Anon's greatest healing effects. We laugh with each other not only because we think we're funny – as often we are – but because we recognize the many aspects of ourselves in each other.'

From Survival To Recovery, Al-Anon Family Groups

Talking to people with similar problems could well provide valuable clues as to which key might fit your drinker's door. For example, we found ourselves discussing uncanny similarities between a drinker we knew and one known by a couple we met at a self-help gathering for friends and families of alcohol abusers. By sharing the approach that had worked for our own alcoholic friend, and advising the couple to try it with their loved one, we directed them to the key that fitted their particular door, and their loved one has been dry ever since. It was extremely satisfying and just goes to show how sharing information really can make a difference.

Some of the potential benefits are similar to those that can be derived from other kinds of networking. Getting out and meeting people who are in the same boat is likely to broaden your knowledge of alcohol issues, provide you with personal recommendations of important books to read and suitable therapists and clinics for your loved one to attend, and keep you up to date with any new medical developments that people are talking about. It might also secure you some good friends and, perhaps most importantly of all, prove vital for your own happiness and wellbeing.

Only those who have gone through what you are going through are likely to be able to understand how you're feeling, and this is one of the things that explains the huge global success of Alcoholics Anonymous, which will also teach you how to live with yourself.

Taking that initial decision to get out and be sociable again may sound intimidating because living with a problem drinker often makes people withdrawn. The stigma of having a partner or member of the family with such a condition can make you wary of mixing with others, as can the realization that people are unlikely to understand or empathize with your situation. If, for example, you have been practising the art of detachment, it could be difficult to explain to those with no knowledge of the subject that the reason you're not actively helping a problem drinker is simply because you care about them so much! Even professional helpers can be largely oblivious to what you have to put up with.

'If at some time or another you, the non-alcoholic spouse, have to deal with members of the helping profession who are trying to be of assistance to your family, you may find that they don't understand, or are unsympathetic to, your situation. Sometimes when these people visit your household what they see is *your* anger. They have no idea of what you've been through with your husband. They don't know that your husband can come off as totally (falsely) charming to the outside world.'

Toby Rice Drews from *Getting Them Sober, Volume 2*

People with the same experiences are more likely to be on the same wavelength and should, therefore, be better able to offer you support in your determination to be detached. The more kindred spirits with whom you can talk about things the better. You may find that a network of people you can talk to is just what you need.

The Same the World Over

All the main points we have made in this chapter will apply regardless of where you live in the world. The pain involved in helping someone you love try to recover from alcohol addiction crosses all geographical boundaries, as do the main considerations involved with coping.

Whilst it is true that different countries are not entirely without their distinguishing features, these are relatively minor in the scale of things. For example, UK mental health legislation does not allow involuntary confinement for alcohol abuse, but in the US this is permitted in certain states. Similarly, family relationships in Australia can differ from those in the UK, as Professor John Saunders, Professor and Consultant Physician in Internal Medicine and Addiction Medicine at the Faculty of Medicine at the University of Sydney, Australia, explains, 'Australians with alcohol dependence tend to be less connected with their families than their counterparts in the UK. They are more likely to be living by themselves in transient accommodation and to become malnourished and suffer the consequences of that, including vitamin deficiency and alcohol-related brain damage. They are less likely to have a family member who is concerned about them. However, where they do have a concerned family member I do not see any particular difference in the issues faced in Australia compared to the UK.'

So, wherever you are based, stop blaming yourself, realize that you are far from being the only one in your situation, make a big effort to be open-minded, involve a third party and try to mix with others facing similar problems. Please also try and be patient, however hard that may sound.

Your loved one didn't get addicted overnight, so it would be unrealistic to expect them to make an instant recovery. It could take them two or even three years to feel they have recovered, and even if the key that works for them provides a more instantaneous solution, it is likely to take a similar length of time before you are convinced that this time the recovery is for real!

■ CASE STUDY It Seemed the Kindest Thing to Do

Despite having shared the same South London home for a decade, forty-year-old local government administrator Dorothy Sawyer admits that it was only during the final stages of her thirteen-year relationship with her ex-husband Paul that she twigged he had a drink problem.

'When we were in our twenties I put it down to his artistic temperament,' she explains. 'Then, when I got unexpectedly pregnant and wanted to knuckle down to prepare to bring up our child and make sure we could pay the bills, I realized he was never pulling in the same direction and was always going out on benders. I don't think I realized the severity of the problem until it started to impact on my own health.

'I had always managed to cope and hold down responsible jobs. In fact, it was work that kept me from falling to pieces. But a year before the end, even though I always went to work, I didn't feel like getting out of bed when I woke up in the morning. At least work was sympathetic when I explained what was going on.'

Dorothy, who finally took the decision to leave Paul five years ago, vividly recalls things coming to a head during a trip to New York three years before the end of their relationship. She had wanted to see as much of the city as possible, but he was obsessed with visiting clubs and bars and staying out late, even if it resulted in spending most of the next day in bed. While visiting a church there she came across leaflets about problem drinking and gave him one. Unfortunately, it didn't have the desired effect: he 'flipped' and wandered off, refusing to discuss the subject.

'When you have been with someone for that long it can be hard to be cruel to them.'

Six months later denial reared its ugly head again when they both attended a family therapy group, which their GP had recommended after Paul went to see him about depression and received a prescription for anti-depressants. The couple found themselves sitting next to a two-way mirror while a team of people watched them interact. Paul blamed Dorothy for his depression, but as soon as she mentioned his drinking he stormed out of the session. When he eventually returned he talked about family history and virtually everything except drink.

A further six months down the line Dorothy's revelation that she had started attending Al-Anon meetings was greeted in much the same vein.

'When I told him I was going he said I must be mental as there was no reason to do so,' she recalls. 'He had been sacked from his job as a designer and the design agency's management had told me that it was because of drink, but he insisted they were being ridiculous and that it was all their problem. They got him into a rehab clinic, but he checked himself out after only a few days.

'He kept on blaming me, accusing me of causing the whole thing by teaming up with the management. Right up until the time that I left he refused to admit to having a drink problem and, even when I gave him an ultimatum a few days before leaving, saying that he had to stop or he was going to ruin our son's life, he refused to give up, saying that he didn't think there was any point.'

'At times I was worried he was going to harm himself. It had all got so bad that, although I know it's a dreadful thing to say, I almost thought it might be a good thing if he did so.'

The night before she left, Dorothy stayed out all night at a party to see how he would react if she behaved in the same way as he did. It was an experiment that, in retrospect, she wishes she hadn't tried as when she got back Paul threatened to kill her and burn the house down. He then assaulted her and was subsequently arrested and taken into custody. Dorothy didn't press charges.

'The police told him to stay away, so he went to live with a friend and eventually found a place of his own,' she continues. 'He was always hassling me and trying to get in touch, so I had to get the police to talk to him again, and they threatened him with an injunction.'

Much to Dorothy's relief, communication then ceased for a sustained period, but two years later she received an email out of the blue saying that he had decided to attend a rehab clinic in Ireland. He wrote her numerous letters during his four-month stay in the clinic and even apologized for his behaviour. He has since been dry for two years, suffering only one relapse, and has even found a new partner and got remarried.

Dorothy, who has also remarried, says, 'Splitting up was possibly the kindest thing to do because when you have been with someone for that long it can be hard to be cruel to them. They take it for granted that they can get away with anything and that you will always be there for them. You are almost treated like a mother towards the end. It was the only realistic option left available to me and it has worked, both for me and for him.

'I think I had subconsciously contemplated taking this course of action for years, but I could never face being without him. At times I was worried he was going to harm himself. It had got so bad that, although I know it's a dreadful thing to say, I almost thought it might be a good thing if he did so.'

In summary

- We urge you to remember that there are hundreds of millions of people worldwide in a similar position to yourself and that you did not cause your friend or loved one's drinking, so please stop feeling guilty

- Remember also that there is an important difference between detaching yourself from somebody and totally disowning them

- Try to meet as many people in similar situations to yourself as possible

- Make sure that you involve a third party from outside 'the system'

- Be open-minded and patient. It may take time to find the key that fits your problem drinker's door, and the recovery process, like the addiction process, can take time

CHAPTER TWO

Understanding the Drinker and Yourself

There are dozens of books that deal with combating alcohol problems, half of which begin with the assertion that alcoholism is an incurable disease, while the other half state that it quite definitely isn't a disease. It's therefore hardly surprising that you have become perplexed or confused about what alcoholism really is.

One major issue contributing to this confusion is that different people can use the term 'alcoholic' to mean very different things. Some use it to refer simply to anyone who finds it difficult to exercise control over their drinking, whilst others reserve it for describing those with a full-blown physical addiction, who would not be able to give up drinking without experiencing severe withdrawal symptoms.

For this reason we prefer to talk about people having 'drink problems', rather than being alcoholics, because we feel there is less scope for ambiguity. The term alcoholic can provide those who are in denial about their drinking with a convenient get-out clause, because they can always think of a reason why they are *not* an alcoholic, unless they are actually sleeping on a park bench. We are still happy to use the word 'alcoholic' in these pages when quoting other experts and authors or when referring to organizations who use the term in their title. We also respect the fact that many sufferers find the word helpful to describe their condition.

I [Edmund] used to constantly come up with such a get-out clause when I was in denial about my drink problem in my twenties. I would, for example, constantly point out that I couldn't possibly be an alcoholic because I couldn't remember the first time I tasted alcohol, and I had heard on the radio that every alcoholic can remember that life-changing moment with the utmost clarity. I used to set great store by the fact that I didn't drink spirits, didn't need an 'eye opener' first thing in the morning and that, during the early years, I could give up drinking alcohol altogether for brief periods.

Such logic is guaranteed to lure drinkers into a false sense of security because, whatever level they are currently drinking at, the body will eventually require more alcohol to create the same effect, making it a decidedly slippery slope. Someone who prides themselves on being able to give up drinking every January, for example, may well find that they soon start giving up only for part of January and that eventually they become unable to give up at all.

'An alcoholic or alcohol abuser in denial can break a family apart or literally kill another person in a drunk driving accident and still not see their *drinking* as a problem. Unless and until alcoholics and alcohol abusers break through their denial, the consequences of their drinking will continue to spiral downward.'

Lisa Frederiksen from *If You Loved Me, You'd Stop!*

There are two basic categories of alcohol addiction – psychological addiction and physical addiction – and the former, if it fails to be addressed, can lead to the latter. Many experts do not distinguish between the two because they feel there is a danger that those who only have a psychological addiction will feel they don't have anything to worry about.

Jeffrey Huttman PhD from Challenges says, 'Common

practice is not to classify an individual as having a psychological addiction and hence conveying that the difficulty may not be problematic in the absence of physiological dependence. Problems with alcohol use can be classified as Alcohol Dependence when there are adverse psychological or physical consequences, or Alcohol Abuse if they have risen to the level of affecting such areas as social, occupational or interpersonal functioning.'

Nevertheless, although we don't have a clinical background, we found ourselves desperately trying to make sense of alcohol issues after experiencing a friend dying as a direct result of a drink problem, and we found the distinction between psychological addiction and physical addiction of fundamental importance in enabling us to develop an understanding of the subject. We therefore feel it is crucial to pass on this information to you, albeit with the caveat that it's essential to realize that anyone with a psychological addiction is still causing themselves harm and in need of help.

One thing we had never managed to understand was why some people with drink problems could never go back to drinking again in the future while others sometimes could, and this was an issue that didn't seem to be explained by anybody we asked or any books on the subject we came across. The answer lies in understanding the difference between a psychological addiction and a physical addiction. So what is the difference?

Physical Addiction

Someone who has developed a physical addiction to alcohol will not be able to stop drinking without getting withdrawal symptoms, which could range from hallucinating or becoming physically sick to sweating, shakiness and becoming argumentative. In some cases withdrawal symptoms may amount to no more than becoming anxious and experiencing disrupted sleep patterns, so they can be hard to identify with certainty.

'Problem drinkers who have gone through withdrawal before are more likely to have withdrawal symptoms each time they stop drinking. Some individuals have the forms of syndrome including tremors, seizures and hallucinations, typically occurring within six to forty-eight hours after the last alcoholic drink. Withdrawals can be mild, moderate or severe. For most problem drinkers, alcohol withdrawal will not progress to the severe stage of delirium tremens (confusion and hallucination).'

G. Hussein Rassool from *Alcohol and Drug Misuse*

Once someone has reached this stage of physical addiction they should not consider stopping drinking suddenly, as to do so could result in memory loss or brain damage. Indeed, it could even kill them. They need to seek medical advice and they may find they need to undergo a medical detox, which will involve having the alcohol replaced by substitute drugs in quantities that will decrease over a period of days. Depending on the circumstances, this detox could be administered at the individual's home, in a rehab clinic or by making regular visits to a GP or hospital.

It is important to bear in mind that once someone has reached this physically addicted state but has not yet detoxed, refusing them the opportunity to drink alcohol could prove extremely dangerous or even fatal.

A thirty-five-year-old former problem drinker told us, 'When a family member or friend, visiting GP or paramedic says they can't possibly give you alcohol you just have to suffer it, but they are potentially giving you a death sentence. I had all three instances of this happening in the same evening when I was having fits. The paramedic prescribed medication, but my mother had to drive over two miles the following day to get it, and the GP was particularly unforgiving about me and my plight. I will never forget her indignation.'

This former drinker stressed that there is a safe way to come off alcohol and, in the absence of a medically supervised detox, an absolute must is to wean a person off alcohol slowly. If they are having a hard time, then look at reducing their intake gradually. 'This has to be measured out by a family member or friend and can be given in the interim whilst awaiting prescription medication or being admitted to a ward. If admission or medication is refused, then this is the only way, from my own hard-learned experience, to avoid damaging someone permanently and potentially allowing them to die.'

Even if someone with no significant withdrawal symptoms is reasonably certain that they don't have a physical addiction, they should leave nothing to chance and should cut down the amount they are drinking gradually over a series of weeks until they're drinking at a safe level.

Detox or no detox, the process of withdrawing from alcohol will only represent the beginning of the recovery process, and it could take as long as a couple of years before problem drinkers feel they are functioning at somewhere towards 'normal'. Furthermore, the majority of alcohol experts will recommend that they should never touch another drop again for as long as they live.

'Those around the alcoholic are forever asking him to "cut down". This is like asking your daughter to get only a little pregnant.'

Dennis Wholey from *The Courage to Change*

The conventional wisdom is that, even if someone has remained dry for several decades, they will revert to drinking at their previous levels almost as soon as they touch their first alcoholic drink because the brain has been permanently altered in a way that will instantly recognize the taste, sensation and smell of alcohol. As we shall see in Chapter 6, however, there are now some modern methods of treatment that can enable those with physical addictions to go back to drinking in moderation. These are obviously hugely controversial because they defy traditional thinking, but they clearly can work in many cases.

The early years of recovery can be especially hard for those with physical addictions because they may experience intense cravings for alcohol, and it is when these cravings occur that they are most likely to relapse, regardless of all the good intentions and resolutions they have expressed. We have heard drinkers liken cravings to the feeling that you are walking through a desert dying of thirst, but knowing there is an oasis (i.e., a pub) around the corner that you can pop into.

Dr Francis Keaney of King's College, London, describes cravings as being a bit like waves on the seashore. They build up slowly, come to a peak and then reduce. In the immediate aftermath there can be very strong cravings, but they reduce in intensity as the drinker becomes alcohol free.

'In general, each craving never lasts longer than twenty minutes,' Keaney says. 'Some drinkers say they have them all the time, but when you ask them about the intensity they then say it builds up to a peak and reduces. During the actual withdrawal phase the cravings break into one another and they seem permanent. Everyone is different and much depends on the person or their pain tolerance.'

The good news is that in the majority of cases the cravings a former drinker experiences should become less of a problem over time. So if you have a friend or loved one who keeps relapsing after only a few months, or even after a whole year of remaining dry, and complains that they simply cannot resist the cravings they experience, it's important to remind them that things should get easier if they can manage to remain on the wagon for longer next time.

Professor Keith Humphreys of Stanford University, USA, points to research by Dr George Vaillant, a professor of Psychiatry at Harvard Medical School, which has shown that if a male alcoholic can go for four years without drinking then the chances of relapsing are no greater than that of a non-drinker developing an alcohol problem in the first place.

Humphreys says, 'Cravings do reduce over time. So although one should be sympathetic about someone's cravings and not deny that there can be a problem, one can also point out that they are something the body has developed as opposed to something that has been present since birth. So they are therefore something they can get rid of if they stop drinking for long enough.'

■ CASE STUDY New Family Makes All the Difference

Like many drinkers who end up with physical addictions, alcohol crept up gradually on forty-five-year-old Carolyn Hughes. During her student days she never drank to be sociable, only to get drunk, and by the age of twenty-four she was binge drinking heavily and was frequently drunk for the entire weekend. During her late twenties she was drinking a bottle of wine or half a bottle of vodka every night of the week.

'At the time I knew I was drinking too much, but I didn't think I had a serious drink problem, even though people at work noticed and took me to one side and said they didn't want me to get into any trouble. I remember, in particular, being horrified when my GP offered to give me a medical detox because I'd thought detoxes were for people on park benches.'

Carolyn, who began drinking alcohol at fifteen, feels that her dependency resulted primarily from the fact that her mother disappeared when she was only three years old, leaving her to be brought up by a father she describes 'as a horrible and evil man'. The experience severely damaged her self-esteem and left her feeling worthless and unloved.

Even when she left home and started working as a social worker in South London, her father's behaviour continued to cause her major problems, so it came as an immense relief when he died of a kidney problem when she was twenty-eight.

At this point she hoped to put all her problems behind her and quit drinking, but unfortunately it didn't prove quite that easy. The low sense of self-worth remained and the amount she was drinking continued to increase.

'At the time I knew I was drinking too much, but I didn't think I had a serious drink problem.'

Whenever someone mentioned her drinking at work it just made her think of better ways to cover it up, such as carrying vodka in Coca-Cola or Fanta bottles. She would arrange meetings on the phone rather than face to face and take work home at every opportunity. If her work duties required her to meet members of the public she would carry around a toothbrush and toothpaste and nip into a public toilet to use them to hide the smell.

After a spell in hospital being treated for a brain tumour at the age of thirty-one, Carolyn reached the point of no return work-wise and was sent home for turning up to work drunk. By then her drinking had become all-consuming, starting with a hair of the dog first thing in the morning, continuing at the pub at lunch-time and regularly being supplemented by vodka from her handbag. Even knowing she had found a boyfriend who loved her didn't prove a strong enough incentive to remain dry. The couple got engaged on the condition that she cut down, but the relationship lasted a mere eighteen months.

'Because he worked as a bouncer, he didn't drink much, so he cottoned on to my drinking within weeks and was always telling me I had a drink problem,' Carolyn recalls. 'He worked out that I'd always had a drink before I met him and this shocked me because I wondered how he could tell, as I thought I was behaving normally. I tried very, very hard to give up alcohol because I knew he loved me, but I couldn't get through a day without a drink. I tried cutting down by monitoring what I was drinking and switching from vodka to wine, but it just didn't work.

'My friends were so delighted I'd found this boyfriend, even though it eventually transpired he wasn't the right one. Most of them knew I drank an awful lot and thought I would drink less because of him. Around that time they would invite us to their places and we would find there was no drink with the meals, which in some ways made things worse as it made me feel guilty and ridiculous. I didn't feel grateful at the time and it didn't help because, although they didn't know it, I always had alcohol with me in my handbag.'

'Even when I invited them to my place they brought Coca-Cola and it annoyed me,' she continues. 'It felt very patronizing and it definitely had a negative effect. In hindsight, I think that the only thing that could have actually helped was if all my friends had got together and said that I had to stop drinking or they weren't going to carry on talking to me. But it might have made me kill myself.'

'They would invite us round and we would find there was no drink with the meals, which in some ways made things worse as it made me feel guilty and ridiculous.'

Carolyn did in fact attempt suicide at the age of thirty-three, even without such a confrontation with her friends. In the absence of the prop of a job, she found little else to do other than drink and began sinking ever more deeply into debt as she downed a litre of vodka, a bottle of wine and six cans of beer every day. She withdrew from socializing with people about a month beforehand and told them she was going on holiday, then she decided to kill herself via an injection of rat poison, but fortunately got too drunk to carry it out. The next morning she was rudely awakened by the sound of her phone ringing.

She had completely forgotten that her GP, having been worried by her depression, had made an appointment for her to see a psychiatrist at the local hospital that morning, and the hospital had phoned to remind her of the appointment. She was afraid that if she didn't turn up they might come round and see the state of her flat!

When she saw the psychiatrist, he immediately sectioned her in a mental hospital, and while she was there, Carolyn discovered, via blood tests, that her liver was badly damaged. She found out about a new rehab initiative, organized by local charity Kenward Trust, called the Naomi Project for women with drink problems, and, after spending six months there, she hasn't touched a drop of alcohol for eleven years.

'I began to understand how I'd been hurt and how I'd hurt others in return,' Carolyn explains. 'I didn't want to drink any more as I was so tired and ashamed of letting people down. Now I'm in recovery I have a choice about my alcoholism, as opposed to when I was drinking, and although I did experience cravings to begin with, it was up to me to get help. The first year was definitely the hardest, not just because of the cravings, but because I had to deal with so much emotional mess and get out of the habit of going for a drink.'

'It was really nice to think someone cared enough to come and visit me in rehab and appreciated what a tough thing I was going through.'

Carolyn, whose liver has now repaired itself, singles out practising the AA's 12 Steps as being key to her having remained sober. The other major factor in her recovery has been her newly acquired family. Six months after leaving rehab she met Brendan, who had also overcome a drink problem a couple of years earlier, and they got married after two years of dating. By 2004 she had given birth to two baby daughters.

'From the moment my girls were born I've lived for them. They are my greatest motivation for staying sober and I never want them to see me drunk. Having such a strong, loving family has enabled me to put the past behind me and I have even managed to forgive my dead father for the way he treated me. My family know they are loved and wanted and that their mother will never disappear!

'I definitely think that the support Brendan and I are able to give to each other has been important for us remaining sober. It's because we are both in recovery and have the same willingness to keep sober that we don't need AA meetings any more, but we both attended AA in our recovery and found it helpful. Sobriety does get easier with time because it stops being an issue and becomes part of your lifestyle, but I definitely think it would be harder to live with someone who drinks occasionally.'

'Thankfully cravings are now minimal,' she continues, 'but when they were a problem I knew that I shouldn't ignore them and should talk to someone about them, so Brendan would be the first person I would discuss the matter with. As a couple, we do discuss situations where alcohol might be an issue, like attending weddings or funerals, and we form a plan for coping. When his family come to stay we buy them their favourite tipple, and that is OK with both of us, but otherwise we don't keep alcohol in the house and don't go to pubs. I think it's common sense to say that if you are going to keep sober you need to keep away from the pub.

'Another necessity has been to create a different social life that doesn't involve alcohol. We go out for the occasional meal, but otherwise our hobbies are home-based. I have found that friends are very supportive once I've told them why I don't drink, so I would suggest to anyone who is trying to stay sober to let everyone know. My life in sobriety is so much better than when I was drinking and I wouldn't want to go back to where I came from. Some days that is incentive enough. No disrespect to Kenward Trust, but I would never want to go to rehab again. It was so tough.'

'I think that the only thing that could have actually helped was if all my friends had got together and said that I had to stop drinking or they weren't going to carry on talking to me. But it might have made me kill myself.'

Carolyn, who now lives in Ireland, acknowledges the fact that having one true friend who came to visit her in rehab made all the difference. Most of her friends 'didn't want to know' when they realized how bad things had become, but having someone who really cared and who realized she was suffering from an addiction rather than lacking self-discipline really helped.

'It was really nice to think someone cared enough to come and visit me in rehab and appreciated what a tough thing I was going through.'

Psychological Addiction

As already discussed, if someone has a psychological addiction to alcohol it doesn't mean they aren't causing themselves any harm. As well as risking liver damage, they risk harming themselves in a number of other different ways, from stomach disorders, high blood pressure and heart problems to cancer, skin disorders, decreased mental functioning and physical accidents.

It's important to realize that those who only drink wine and beer can cause themselves just as much harm as those who drink spirits. What matters is the actual amount of alcohol you consume, not the type of drink.

Anyone who drinks for reasons other than simply enjoying the experience is forming an adverse psychological relationship with alcohol. A classic example of this is if someone comes home from work and uses alcohol as a prop to relieve stress.

Classic signs of a psychological addiction include drinking at the same time each day and starting to put alcohol before other things. If, for example, someone puts drink before their partner or turns down invitations to events or places because they know they won't be able to fuel their appetite for alcohol to the extent that they'd like, they probably fall into this category.

Someone with a psychological addiction will not normally experience the more serious types of withdrawal symptoms associated with a physical addiction because, although they need alcohol to function normally and feel good, their body has not yet adapted to chronic use of the drug. They may, however, still experience disturbed sleep patterns and feel anxious and moody. Someone with a psychological addiction may be able to go back to drinking in moderation again in the future, but there is much to be said for them going dry for an initial period in order to examine their unhealthy relationship with alcohol and work out how to deal with it.

The boundaries between a psychological and physical addiction are extremely blurred and many drinkers fall into the grey area between the two, when it's clear they have a psychological addiction, but unclear whether they have a physical addiction as well. Furthermore, the term alcoholic, which in its purest sense refers to someone with a physical addiction, is frequently used to refer to those with psychological addictions, too, even though they can give up for brief periods without experiencing withdrawal symptoms.

'Most alcoholics, unless they're in the later stages of addiction, are capable of cutting back for periods of time. In the early and middle stages of addiction, the alcoholic doesn't lose complete control over his alcohol or other drug use. Instead he has periodic loss of control. For example, an alcoholic may cut back to two beers a day for a month. Then, one day, he can't stop at two beers and loses control.'

Jeff Jay and Debra Jay from *Love First*

Does the Drinker Have a Disease?

As the term alcoholic can be used to refer to people suffering from markedly different degrees of addiction, it's no great surprise that there is widespread disagreement regarding whether or not an alcoholic is suffering from a disease. Our own view is that when someone is at the psychological addiction stage it's unhelpful to label them as having a disease, because doing so can prevent them from making sufficient efforts to overcome their drink problem, put it behind them and move on.

If, on the other hand, they are suffering from the worst kind of physical addiction, then we think that regarding the condition as a disease can be helpful to the drinker, as it makes them realize they have become powerless against alcohol because their brain chemistry has changed. It's also helpful to their loved ones as it allows them to detach and realize there may be little more that they can do to help.

Whether a drinker is considered to be suffering from a disease or not isn't the important issue, though. If you choose to call it a disease, then that's fine, as long as you're happy. The important thing is not what you call it, it's realizing what you can do to help.

Theories propounded by experts go well beyond merely whether those with drink problems have a disease. One school of thought cites a strong genetic link, while others focus on social, cultural or psychoanalytical factors. Indeed, you can make very few generalizations in this field without provoking opposition from some quarters. For example, the assertion made by many that no one ever consciously sets out to be an alcoholic is an extremely useful starting point for dealing with the subject of blame.

Peter Smith, Head of Counselling at Broadway Lodge rehab clinic in Weston-super-Mare in Somerset, says, 'It's not your fault that someone has turned to drink, but neither is it the drinker's fault. As soon as you get into judgement you start with arguments and blame. If you take the attitude that its no one's fault then it creates a level playing field. But that doesn't mean there isn't an element of accountability or responsibility in there.'

In *Games Alcoholics Play*, Claude Steiner presents a theory that people can consciously set out to develop a drink problem. It's based on the notion that some people make conscious decisions in childhood or early adolescence that influence and make predictable the rest of their lives. Those whose lives are based on such decisions are said to have a script.

'Like diseases, scripts have an onset, a course and an outcome. Because of this similarity, scripts have been mistaken for diseases. However, because scripts are based on consciously willed decisions rather than on morbid tissue changes, they can be revoked or "undecided" by similarly willed decisions.'

Claude Steiner from *Games Alcoholics Play*

Opinion can be deeply divided even on something as fundamental as the hereditary link. There is substantial evidence to show that drink problems run in families, but experts disagree on the proportion of drinkers whose problems have been caused or exacerbated by such genetic factors. Some say it's a third whilst others say it's half. But it's also equally clear that many people develop drink problems when there's no history of excessive drinking in their immediate family.

Rather than getting unduly bogged down with academic theory, a good starting point is to realize that there can be many different types of drink problems resulting from many different causes. Furthermore, some of these causes may overlap. Just because someone has a genetic predisposition to developing a drink problem doesn't automatically mean they will develop one. But if this predisposition is combined with other factors, such as memories of childhood abuse, a relationship breakdown or an unmanageable workload, then the chances of addiction occurring become very much greater.

Additionally, just as there can be a number of different underlying factors contributing towards a drink problem, there can be a number of different treatment methods required for overcoming it. For example, even if your drinker has managed to go dry without using the 12 Step approach, they may find that attending AA provides them with valuable social interaction in the early stages of their recovery. They may also have underlying psychological issues that need to be dealt with via specialist counselling at the same time.

So let's stop thinking in terms of seeing everything as black and white, even if other sources of help you have considered may urge you to do so. If you have read that confrontation doesn't work, that's not necessarily true. As we will see in Chapter 4, although it's a high-risk strategy, it certainly can work in some cases. Conversely, it's also true that some of the most effective strategies used to get drinkers to realize they need to seek help set great store on avoiding confrontation.

If you are trying to help a drinker, we suggest that your energy would be much better spent attempting to work out which approach would be most appropriate for you to try first in your particular case, rather than coming to conclusions about whether any one approach is necessarily 'better' than another.

Look out for the lies

There are a few useful generalizations that can be made about those who have developed the most serious kinds of drink problems. They are normally using alcohol as a form of anaesthetic and they are usually in denial about their drinking and constantly tell lies.

Keith Burns, Managing Director of ADMIT Services, a national intermediary that specializes in arranging treatment packages for those with alcohol problems, says, 'It is important when dealing with an alcohol misuser not to believe that what they are telling you is entirely accurate. You have to read between the lines; when they say it was some major event that turned them to drink, such as the death of a loved one or a messy divorce, it is simply their "excuse" for drinking. You normally find that it was the drinking that caused the marriage break-up and not the other way round.'

Burns points out that an alcohol misuser will find almost any excuse for their drinking. 'I lost my job', probably means they turned up for work the worse for wear, and 'I had a terrible car accident' may mean they were driving under the influence. Furthermore, drinkers are unlikely to recover for the benefit of someone else. They must want to do it for themselves, so constantly nagging them and telling them they drink too much won't help. If anything it's likely to make things worse. It can be more effective to say how the drinker's behaviour makes you feel, i.e., it makes you feel afraid, sad, hurt or unloved.

The key starting point for anyone to want to instigate their own recovery is, of course, for them to realize that they have a problem to recover from. Once again, whether they choose to regard this problem as a disease is something of a side issue.

'Just as someone else can't force us to get clean and sober in the first place, we can't be made to believe that we are an alcoholic or an addict, either. We have to self-diagnose. We can tell people what they want to hear, but unless we actually believe it, it doesn't make a blind bit of difference. Before we can successfully treat our disease, we have to fully admit to ourselves that we actually have one to begin with.'

Georgia W from *Don't Let the Bastards Grind You Down*

Once an addiction has progressed to a physical addiction, or to the more serious end of the psychological addiction scale, the drinker is effectively using alcohol as an anaesthetic to deaden pain. Its qualities for achieving this aim on a temporary basis are indisputable. After all, before modern-day anaesthetic was invented alcohol was used by medical professionals to deaden pain during amputations and other major operations.

In some cases drinkers are literally combating physical pain – many people with bad backs, for example, have turned to drink as a means of coping – but such physical pain will normally be accompanied by psychological pain as well, and in the majority of cases the pain is entirely psychological.

Indeed, experts commonly point to a huge overlap between drink problems and mental health issues. Alcohol misuse can be both a *cause* of depression – because alcohol depresses the activity of the brain – and a *consequence* of depression. So there can often be something of a chicken and egg situation, in which it's not entirely clear whether the depression or the alcohol abuse started first, because the two can so easily feed off each other.

Keith Burns says, 'Virtually every alcoholic has some form of depression or anxiety. The illness makes them feel different to a non-alcoholic and the alcohol makes them feel normal, despite causing extremely abnormal behaviour.'

The realization that nothing must be allowed to get in the way of accessing this anaesthetic can lead the drinker to construct an elaborate web of lies to disguise their dependency. At a lunch with family or friends, for example, they can often be seen sipping a glass of wine with great moderation, but what nobody realizes is that they are knocking back large quantities of spirits when they leave the room, ostensibly to visit the toilet or answer a call on their mobile.

'It is consumed by 90 per cent of UK adults. But few stop to question their assumptions about booze. The media don't help when they circulate misleading phrases such as "alcohol and drugs". A better expression would be "alcohol and other drugs" – or just "drugs" – because alcohol is a drug.'

Allen Carr from No More Hangovers

If they aren't in their own home they'll more than likely have a secret supply of spirits with them, smuggled inside a handbag or coat pocket. They may well be cleverly disguised in fruit juice containers, and they may even take them out in front of you while you're taking a walk together and pretend to be innocently swigging a soft drink.

But, somewhat strangely, this secrecy and cunning can often be accompanied by blatant demonstrations of drunkenness that nobody in their right minds could possibly think would go undetected. It is, for example, quite common to see someone protesting that they aren't drunk whilst staggering around and slurring their words so badly you can barely make out what they're saying.

Occasionally we used to stay with an ageing family friend who had developed a serious drink problem. She would go to huge lengths to disguise her drinking by, for example, always insisting on paying for lunch when eating out at the local pub. This gave her an excuse to spend a few moments on her own when standing at the bar, during which time she would order and knock back a treble whisky.

Oddly, this secrecy often occurred the night after she had been so drunk she'd fallen down the stairs in full view of her visitors or sung her heart out in a drunken stupor in front of the television. On one occasion, when football legend Jimmy Greaves appeared on the television, she even volunteered in a disgusted voice, 'Do you realize that Jimmy Greaves was an alcoholic?' While another time she revealed, with equal disgust, that her brother-in-law was an alcoholic.

So if you're wondering how anyone in their right mind can behave like that, therein lies the answer. They are not in their right mind. The individual has changed. Whereas before they may have put your love or friendship before most other things, now it will be alcohol that takes first place – before you and before anybody or anything else. The compulsion to drink has become so overwhelming that, even though they may periodically make promises to quit, they are, in fact, powerless to carry out their good intentions without medical help.

The guilt they experience invariably gets projected on to those closest to them. In some cases low self-esteem may have driven them to drink in the first place, while in other cases it may not have done. Whatever the case, by the time they have reached this stage in the addiction chain, low self-esteem will definitely have become a major personality trait. This may well manifest itself through the expression of unrealistically big ideas and absurd gestures of generosity that are completely inappropriate to their means.

The letter opposite, which is used as an educational tool to help families of seriously addicted drinkers understand their condition, summarizes many of these points admirably. It was provided by Bristol-based charity Addiction Recovery Agency (ARA) and is reproduced here with its permission.

AN OPEN LETTER TO MY FAMILY

I am an addict. I need help.

Don't solve my problem for me. This only makes me lose respect for you and for myself.

Don't lecture, moralize, scold, blame or argue, whether I'm drunk or sober. It may make you feel better, but it makes the situation worse.

Don't accept my promises. The nature of my illness prevents me from keeping them, even though I mean them at the time. Promises are my only way of postponing pain. And don't keep switching agreements; if an agreement is made, stick to it.

Don't lose your temper with me. It will destroy you and any possibility of helping me.

Don't let your anxiety for me make you do what I should do for myself.

Don't believe everything I tell you. Often, I don't even know the truth, let alone tell it.

Don't cover up or try and spare me the consequences of my drinking. It may reduce the crisis, but it will make my illness worse.

Above all, don't run away from reality as I do. Alcohol dependence, my illness, gets worse as my drinking continues.

Start now to learn, to understand, to plan for recovery. Find Al-Anon or any organization that exists to help families in your situation.

I need help – from a doctor, a psychologist, a counsellor, from some people in a self-help programme who've recovered from a drink problem themselves, and from a power greater than myself.

Thank you for listening,

An Addict

Looking After Yourself and the Children

Much of the above may seem like preaching to the converted if you have a problem drinker in your life. Nevertheless, you are likely to be far less aware of the real harm that the drinker's behaviour has caused to yourself or to any children that may be involved.

The chances are that you have been suffering in similar ways to the drinker. Your life is likely to have become centred around alcohol and you will probably have developed a very low sense of self-worth and be indulging in a fair amount of self-pity. Like the drinker, you may be shunning contact with others and living in a constant state of fear and anxiety, frequently misinterpreting opinions expressed by others as personal attacks. You have literally been damaged by the behaviour of your loved one.

Just as the drinker tries to blame others for their condition, so the drinker's family members often blame other, largely unrelated things that have gone wrong on the drinker's behaviour. Different members of the family often try to shift the blame for the drinker's state between one another as they find it hard to accept that their own flesh and blood has lost their way and sunk to such a level. The drinker's parents could, for example, try and blame the drinker's spouse for not appearing to care enough.

Getting sucked into covering up for a drinker can prove particularly stressful. Even something as minor as phoning their workplace to say they won't be coming to work because they are ill can create guilt, and you could find yourself faced with some really serious moral dilemmas.

What, for example, should you do if you suspect a friend or family member of driving without a licence after they were banned because of drink-driving? The drinker might tell you that they have got their licence back, but you may know deep down that the amount they're drinking makes it most unlikely that they'd be able to pass a blood test to make this possible. Should you inform the authorities? You may feel it's not appropriate to take such action against someone you're close to, but what if they killed someone while driving under the influence? Would you be able to live with the knowledge that you had effectively caused someone's death by turning a blind eye?

'The feelings of anger, shame, and guilt associated with family alcoholism come from the constant confusion, conflict, unpredictability, inconsistency, mistrust and sense of failure that each member experiences. The family victims seldom learn without outside help that they didn't cause the disease and that they can't control it.'

Evelyn Leite from *Detachment*

For these reasons there is an increasing acceptance amongst alcohol addiction experts that treating those close to problem drinkers should be just as high a priority as treating the drinkers themselves. Indeed, Don Lavender, Programme Director of Camino Recovery on the Costa del Sol in Spain, who has worked in the industry for over thirty years and been an international consultant since 1993, believes that any programme that doesn't offer a family component as part of its care is only half a programme at best.

'I'm not talking about family therapy, I'm talking about family education,' he says. 'Hazelden in the US, which has done residential treatment since 1949, discovered over three decades ago that people in rehab who experienced a "family" component in their care had a 65 per cent higher probability of getting well and staying well.'

When you love someone, or like them a lot, you tend to give them the benefit of the doubt over and over again. But by doing so, and by constantly giving them emotional support, money and helping them out of difficult situations, you invariably end up unintentionally 'enabling' them by shielding them from having to face the consequences of their own behaviour.

'When someone important to us is in trouble, we do what we can to come to her rescue. It's a normal reaction. The strength of families is often measured by their ability to rally in a time of crisis. When a loved one has more than his share of problems, we explain the breakdown in many ways: bad luck, immaturity, rebelliousness, lack of self-discipline, stress, youthful inexperience, or low self-esteem. We surely don't leap to the conclusion that addiction is the source of the problem.'

Jeff Jay and Debra Jay from *Love First*

Esther Harris, Families and Carers Services Co-ordinator at Developing Health and Independence (DHI), a drugs and alcohol charity based in the south west of England, says, 'Mutuality and reciprocity are important to a certain degree in human relation-ships, but someone can become unhealthily co-dependent when they lose a sense of self because they need approval, whatever the cost. A family member with the best intentions may "help" and feel good about doing so, but their behaviour only enables the addict to continue their destructive behaviour. Examples can include paying off debts, making excuses to employers and friends and allowing themselves to believe that they are the reason a loved one drinks.'

Harris highlights that most people are very upset to find out that their attempts to protect their loved one from the worst excesses of their behaviour are in fact enabling it to continue. This process can happen over a long period of time, with the family member eventually feeling as helpless, powerless and hopeless as the addict. She emphasizes that changes are possible, but that they will probably require professional support.

'Family members learn that, although challenging a loved one's behaviour can risk their disapproval and anger, they can also act to support their loved one into treatment and beyond,' she continues. 'When the family member gradually learns about the nature of co-dependency, it makes it possible not only for them to recover themselves, but also to help the addict seek help.'

If a problem drinker has children, then the harm caused can be more far-reaching still. The children can develop a very low sense of self-worth and, if their issues are not addressed, these can manifest as behavioural problems that last into adulthood and which can then be passed down through the generations. They are also far more likely to develop drink problems themselves.

Professor Griffith Edwards, Emeritus Professor of Addiction Behaviour at the National Addiction Centre, Institute of Psychiatry, King's College London, says, 'Children are enormously vulnerable. The mother may not be able to talk to the children if they are always hearing screaming and shouting as a result of their father having a drink problem. They may identify with their father and hold it against their mother. Confidence and trust may be shot to hell by the two most loving people in their lives being in conflict.'

It is common for children of problem drinkers to experience feelings of loneliness and, because they have grown up in relative chaos, to have no experience of what is and is not normal. They can often find it hard to form intimate relationships, tend to put on a skilful front to disguise their fear of having no one to turn to and habitually tell lies. Indeed, research conducted by US author Janet Geringer Woititz into children from alcoholic homes found that they had lost their sense of what was true and what wasn't.

'What was real and what was unreal got very distorted in your household. So there's not a whole lot in it for you to tell the truth. And what happened for a while is that you started lying automatically. And since you didn't feel that you were lying, because everybody's lying, you didn't feel too guilty about it. You may even have fooled yourself into believing you were protecting your family.'

Janet Geringer Woititz from *Adult Children of Alcoholics*

Such children are also more likely than average to have suffered abuse. Research carried out by author Robert J. Ackerman for his book *Perfect Daughters* found that daughters of problem drinkers often found parents with drink problems to be offensive to them – 31 per cent of adult daughters experienced physical abuse as children, 19 per cent were the victims of sexual abuse and 38 per cent witnessed spousal abuse in their families. These rates were three or four times higher than those raised in families without drink problems

In Chapters 7 and 8, we describe in some detail the steps that both loved ones and children of problem drinkers can take to help themselves recover from their predicaments. But, as with those seeking to recover from drink problems, half the battle is acknowledging that you have a problem in the first place.

■ CASE STUDY Mother and Son Both Benefit From Self-Help Groups

Sixty-three-year-old Maggs Horne comes across as surprisingly positive and relaxed for someone whose life had been completely turned upside down by her late husband Jake's drinking.

With him permanently unable to hold down jobs, and frequently becoming violent and disappearing off with other women, she had been forced to return to work as a part-time teacher in order to provide for their son Pete almost single-handedly. Indeed, after twenty years of marriage things had got so bad that the couple finally separated. However, that did not prevent them from staying in touch and from participating in family gatherings in a friendly way.

'He was still my son's father,' explains Maggs, 'and I always had the dream that he might go dry and that I was going to be there for him. But I'd decided I wouldn't tolerate any more unacceptable behaviour. When he was drinking, nothing I said or did ever made any difference and, although he would occasionally go dry for periods of a few months, it never lasted for more than a year.'

Unfortunately the dream died when Jake failed to survive complications to a punctured lung caused by an alcohol-related accident, but both his wife and son were at his deathbed to say goodbye without any bitterness. This is because they had both learned from attending Al-Anon and Alateen – the version of Al-Anon for those aged under twenty – that Jake had been sick as opposed to wilfully bad.

Maggs started going to Al-Anon meetings at the age of twenty-eight – three years after meeting her husband – and she still attends regularly. Pete, who is now thirty-two and has three children, attended Alateen between the ages of eight and fourteen. Maggs is in no doubt that their attendance was the primary reason they were both able to enjoy such a loving relationship with a man most other people had completely rejected.

'Al-Anon helped me see the positives of the relationship,' she enthuses, 'and even now it helps me see that I had many happy years with Jake when he wasn't drinking. It's better to have loved and lost than never to have loved at all. Attending the meetings has taught me to appreciate the good things in life and to realize that every situation has good points and bad points.

'We can't change others, but we can change our attitudes and look for the positives.'

It has taught me to accept that there are things that I can't change. We can't change others, but we can change our attitudes and look for the positives. Even living by oneself can have its advantages. It's not my dream, but Al-Anon has made me realize that there are lots of good things to enjoy.

I have a really happy life, a lovely family with a son and three grandchildren.'

'Alateen helped Pete understand that his father was sick and stopped him from being angry and resentful about his drinking,' continues Maggs. 'You see many adults today who are very resentful of and bitter about the fact that one of their parents was an alcoholic, but attending Alateen prevented him from developing a chip on his shoulder, because he accepts that his father did love him and did the best he could for him. When I see Pete now with his three children he's great and seems to have a healthy, normal parental relationship with them, but lots of children of alcoholics have difficulty forming relationships in adulthood because of the anger they felt in their childhood.'

'There are plenty of people who attend who aren't religious as it's a spiritual programme rather than a religious one.'

'Al-Anon meetings all tend to be a bit different, so I make a point of attending a few different groups. Some people get turned off by the references to God, but you don't need to have any religious beliefs. You just need to acknowledge that there is a power greater than yourself, which can be the Al-Anon group or simply a power for the good. There are plenty of people who attend who aren't religious as it's a spiritual programme rather than a religious one.'

In summary

- A drinker with a physical addiction will experience withdrawal problems, and conventional wisdom says that they should never drink again. They are usually in denial and constantly telling lies, and will put drink before you or anything else

- A person with a drink problem must want to recover for themselves, not for the benefit of others, and the first step is for them to realize they have a problem to recover from

- You must realize that you may also have a problem to recover from, and treating yourself should be as high a priority as treating the drinker

CHAPTER THREE

Helping Someone Cut Down

I f the drinker clearly has a physical addiction then this chapter is not for you, so give it a miss and skip onto the next one. As we have explained in detail in Chapter 2, the conventional wisdom amongst alcohol experts is that anyone who has a physical addiction should never touch another drop because, as soon as they do, they will automatically revert to drinking at the levels they originally drank at.

Jeffrey Huttman PhD from Challenges says, 'There are schools of thought that believe in moderating problem drinking. However, best practice for an individual who has experienced significant past problems as a result of drinking is to become entirely abstinent. I do not recommend that a loved one support the notion of cutting down on drinking, as this often perpetuates the problem and the individual would have already been likely to do so if they were able. Past history of difficulty with addiction or abuse is often the best indicator of what the future will bring.'

There are certainly 'harm reduction' courses that drinkers who have undergone medical detoxes will find they are welcome to try in order to help them drink more moderately once they have undergone an initial dry spell. In some countries these are available free on the state. However, the success rates tend to be very poor and the few who do experience any kind of success probably never had a physical addiction in the first place. They may have had a detox as a sensible precaution but, as we have explained in Chapter 2, the boundaries between the most serious kinds of psychological addictions and the mildest forms of physical addictions are extremely blurred.

> 'He doesn't understand that he has no control over his behaviour when he is drunk. He promises, because he really loves his family and wants to keep his job, that he will stop drinking. He is not lying. He really means it when he says it. But he does not have a choice. So he disappoints himself and everyone who cares about him or needs him. This makes him feel very guilty. Unable to confront the pain, he must ease it, and consequently he drinks some more. This makes him feel even more guilty.'
>
> Janet Geringer Woititz from *Marriage on the Rocks*

Why, then, do those who run such courses invite seriously addicted drinkers to take part when they know they are unlikely to offer any permanent improvement? The answer is that they realize many people simply cannot cope with being confronted with the news that they will never be able to drink again. But if, by trying and failing, they can gradually be brought to the realization that cutting down is never going to work for them, the chances of success are greater.

Our view is that, if you know a physically addicted drinker who simply cannot countenance the idea of giving up alcohol altogether, you would be better off introducing them, in conjunction with suitable medical advice, to some of the newer methods that can enable physically addicted drinkers to go back to drinking in moderation (see Chapter 6).

If you know someone with a psychological addiction who is not in denial about their drinking, you will probably find this chapter extremely helpful. If, on the other hand, you know a drinker who has a psychological addiction but is in denial, then you should jump forward to Chapter 4 and consider the range of methods outlined that can be used to help a drinker come to the realization that they have a drink problem and that they need to seek medical advice.

You Can Help

Whether it be a work colleague who confides in you that they realize they are drinking three or four times the government's recommended guidelines and have decided to cut down, or a friend or family member who has confessed that they are drinking too much too often, the chances are that you can do a lot to help.

Experts commonly stress to those trying to cut down the importance of having the support of those around them. Partners, in particular, have a crucial role to play, especially in terms of offering non-judgemental support and positive feedback. If your partner has a drink problem it's important that you establish exactly what they need to do to help the situation and that you demonstrate a continued interest in their progress, but without acting as some form of policing mechanism.

'He or she doesn't have to have brilliant ideas or fix problems for you. In fact, tell your partner you just want him or her to listen as you share your experiences...A partner could share in the rewards you give yourself. Your partner could actually give you the reward, or you could enjoy it together (or both).'

William R. Miller and Ricardo F. Munoz from
Controlling Your Drinking

You should, however, realize that you might have to make significant changes to your own life in order to help your partner. If your relationship is strong the problem should not prove insurmountable, but it might require a fair amount of work.

Julie Breslin, Service Manager for the Glasgow West area of national charity Addaction, says, 'Partners may well miss drinking with their other half on a Friday night. They may need to make a lot of compromises, and this can be a really hard shift because the bulk of their weekday conversation was probably over a bottle of wine, and they may not have started to open up to each other until they'd had a couple of glasses. The couple often have to put their heads together and rearrange meal times and other routines associated with their previous drinking habits.'

■ CASE STUDY The Company You Keep Can Make All the Difference

For the last nine months Curtis Medwell, a thirty-three-year-old journalist from Manchester, has been recording his daily alcohol intake on his kitchen calendar in a determined attempt to cut down to somewhere near the Government's safe drinking guidelines.

The UK Government recommends that men should drink no more than twenty-one 'units' of alcohol a week and women no more than fourteen (half a pint of standard beer or lager amounting to one unit and one small glass of ordinary strength wine amounting to one and a half units). Curtis aims to keep his weekly total to around twenty-five units a week, but acknowledges that he doesn't manage to do this every week.

'What's been most interesting to me is that I now realize I must have been drinking between forty and sixty units a week in my twenties, when I thought I was drinking thirty units a week,' he admits. 'I don't think most people are honest enough with themselves about how much they actually drink because they will count any pint they drink as two units when it should actually be 2.8 units for 5 per cent beer, and they tend to count any glass of wine as one and a half units when it should be three units for a large glass.

'If you're honest with yourself about what you are drinking and you try and stick to the national guidelines of twenty-one units a week, it's actually quite tough. If you go out for drinks at weekends and spend a night in a bar, it's not hard to drink four pints. That doesn't even feel particularly excessive to me if you do it over four hours, yet if you do that twice in a weekend you've already bust your weekly limit.'

Curtis is in no doubt that the single biggest influence in enabling him to stick to this tough new regime is the support of his thirty-year-old wife Tina, a fellow journalist whom he started dating four years ago. She has also cut down on her drinking and the couple have both quit drinking alcohol altogether during January simply to prove to themselves that they can.

'The fact that she doesn't lecture me is great. She helps me try and be better and points out that it's a journey, not a step change that we're implementing overnight.'

'Sometimes I beat myself up when I add it all up and realize I haven't had as good a week as I thought, and she's always great at picking me up and showing me the progress I've made, and helping me make plans to work a bit harder next week,' explains Curtis. 'I think knowing that we are in it together helps, and the fact that she doesn't lecture me is great. She helps me try and be better and points out that it's a journey, not a step change that we're implementing overnight.

'I'm already drinking much less than I was a year ago and I plan to keep on cutting down further. In particular, I'm getting better about not drinking at all on weekday nights, and the good thing is that we both feel the same pressures. We both really like the idea of rewarding ourselves with a drink when we've had a tough day, and we both always want to say yes to that extra drink that a friend offers down the pub. But we've shown that we can resist those temptations, and I think seeing the other one being disciplined helps us to do the same.

'The most important thing is that it's always a live issue in our house,' he continues. 'We're always talking about how much we're drinking and keeping an eye on it. That way there is no denial and are no surprises. We're honest with ourselves and each other, and that makes it easier to cut down.'

'We've shown that we can resist those temptations, and I think seeing the other one being disciplined helps us to do the same.'

Curtis's decision to largely avoid work-related parties and functions has also greatly assisted his bid to cut down on drinking. The pressure to drink during the early years of his career was immense as his boss made it clear that he expected him to attend virtually every industry party that took place. Now he tends to meet his contacts for lunch and coffee and he never drinks at lunchtime.

'There was always so much free alcohol on offer,' he recalls, 'and back then there were a lot more long boozy lunches. Drinking was part of the culture; everyone was egging you on and if you weren't drinking you were considered a bore. I think that being in a long-term relationship helped me break out of the party scene. It was too tempting to spend my life drifting from one party to the next, where someone else was picking up the bill. But it's quite hard to hold down a relation-ship if you're out drinking with your colleagues every night. In the end, I made a choice to invest in time with my partner, and I'm glad I did.'

A Listening Ear

Friends and acquaintances can also have important parts to play without necessarily having to significantly alter their own lives. When an individual has committed to making a major change like severely cutting down their alcohol intake it's natural to want to share it with someone else, so a listening ear is likely to be much appreciated. Support groups and self-help manuals designed to help people cut down their drinking tend to place great emphasis on drinkers distracting themselves when they feel like having a drink, and phoning a friend for a brief chat is normally high on the list of recommended distractions.

> 'When you're feeling the urge for a drink and want to delay it, distract yourself. If you can put off the urge and that drink for just five minutes and get involved in something else, chances are you'll forget about it for at least ten or fifteen minutes.'
>
> Donna J. Cornett from *7 Weeks to Safe Social Drinking*

The considerations involved with assisting someone who is aware that they are drinking too much are very different to those involved with helping someone in denial. As we explain in Chapter 4, turning up to supper at the home of a drinker in denial with a bottle of fruit juice or Coca-Cola can have exactly the opposite effect to that intended. It can seem terribly patronizing to the drinker and, by winding them up, you will probably make them want to drink more.

You are normally playing an entirely different ball game when someone has acknowledged that they need to take corrective action and has asked for your help. Furthermore, because the majority of these individuals tend to be at the lighter end of the psychological addiction scale, the courses of action you can help them implement have a greater chance of succeeding than they do with the more seriously addicted. Indeed, in some cases you might have to do literally no more than volunteer support and listen occasionally for the drinker to pretty much solve the problem on their own.

Dr Alex Wodak of St Vincent's Hospital says, 'Family and friends should avoid trying to discuss the matter when the drinker is intoxicated, but they should let the problem drinker know they are happy to help. It is important to realize that a substantial proportion of people struggling with excessive alcohol, tobacco, prescription or illicit drug consumption gain control of the situation through their own devices.'

However, there may still be occasions when their drinking annoys you, especially if they are binge drinkers, and you may feel you need to communicate this to them. If so, some of the considerations involved are similar to those when dealing with someone in denial.

Madeleine Moore, who runs WorkScales Ltd and is a qualified counsellor/coach, stresses that, as with someone in denial, the key message is to tell them how their bad behaviour affected you personally, as opposed to criticizing them. For example, you could ask them whether they were aware that they woke you up at two o'clock in the morning and had an argument with you, and you could explain that you were worried they might get beaten up if they carried on behaving like that. Indeed, she knows someone who has given up alcohol altogether because of this feedback.

Moore says, 'So long as you concentrate on behaviour and on how it affects you personally they can't argue with you. If, on the other hand, you criticize or nag, you become the enemy. You can instead try and distract the person and get them involved with something more meaningful.'

She recommends taking them for a walk or to see friends, introducing them to a gym or evening class or other group in the area or, if they are a work colleague, telling them about industry-related seminars or lectures that take place after work. In all these cases you can actually offer to go with them for company, but she points out that it must be something they are actually interested in, because a lot of people drink when they're bored.

It is also important to be aware of the fact that some people who appear to be owning up to very mild drink problems might actually be more serious drinkers attempting to camouflage the extent of their problems. For this reason it's important that if they decide they need to have a dry spell before cutting down, you don't advise them to suddenly stop drinking altogether. As explained in Chapter 2, if they do have a physical addiction this could cause them serious memory loss or brain damage and could even prove fatal.

Advise them instead to cut down their alcohol intake gradually. If, for example, they are drinking fifteen cans of beer a day they should look to reduce this to a couple of cans a day over a number of weeks. According to experts there is much to be said for encouraging someone to stick to one type of drink when cutting down, as it makes it easier to monitor the quantity of alcohol being consumed.

Spotting the Warning Signs

Exactly what you can or should do to help someone wishing to cut down will depend to a large extent on what stage their drinking career has reached. When alarm bells first start ringing it's quite possible that you may recognize all is not well before the drinker does. This does not mean the drinker is in denial, but it does mean they haven't yet given the matter due consideration. It's therefore commonly known by experts as the 'pre-contemplative stage'.

People won't arrive at such a situation overnight. Indeed, it might take many months to develop. In some cases they may start drinking more heavily than normal because of a specific event, such as losing a job or splitting up with a partner, and this is not necessarily a big deal because they may well soon come to the realization that they need to sort themselves out. If, however, they fail to snap out of it after two or three months, there could be cause for concern.

'We glamorize and emphasize the illusory benefits. One of the unfortunate features of icebergs is that 90 per cent of them is hidden beneath the surface. With alcoholism, 99.99 per cent of the problem is hidden. There is a stigma attached to being a pathetic alcoholic instead of a "happy" drinker in complete control, so we are all forced to lie about our problem.'

Allen Carr from *Easy Way to Control Alcohol*

Much depends on the individual circumstances concerned, but those who continue to drink heavily for much longer than two or three months are likely to start showing tell-tale signs of being late for work or looking scruffy. They may often need the additional support of talking to a suitably qualified professional, and those closest to them may need to point out the availability of such an option.

If, for example, they have experienced the death of a loved one, they may well need the help of a bereavement counsellor. If, on the other hand, they are suffering from stress at work then they may need help developing problem-solving or anxiety-management skills so they can deal with stress without resorting to drinking. If their employer has an employee assistance programme (EAP), it could well be appropriate to point this out to them.

Employee Assistance Programmes

A significant number of large companies worldwide now offer EAPs, which can provide employees with free confidential counselling, both over the phone or face-to-face. Although these deal with a wide range of stress-related problems, they originated in the US specifically for the purposes of combating alcohol addiction, and can be particularly effective in preventing early-stage drink problems from developing into full-blown absenteeism issues.

Most good EAPs will provide a professional counsellor or psychologist who can help the drinker understand the issues behind their use of alcohol as a coping mechanism. If a problem has become very serious, they can also refer the employee to alcohol addiction specialists.

Eugene Farrell, secretary of the Employee Assistance European Forum (EAEF), says, 'EAPs can introduce drinkers to alternative coping mechanisms. If, for example, they are drinking because of a workload problem or because of a relationship problem at work, their counsellor can help them understand that they can talk to their HR department or their line manager in order to deal with the problem rather than avoid it.'

Farrell also emphasizes that employees who seek out help tend to show much more commitment than those who are referred by line managers, so work colleagues should give drinkers a gentle nudge in the right direction to show they are supportive of them. He points out that being a good colleague and friend is all about nudging someone towards a proven tool, but the key is not to lay it on too thick, as that can create resistance.

If there is no obvious trigger for the drinking then you may find that you can do little more at this pre-contemplative stage than provide them with basic information on the dangers of drinking and some of the more general sources of help available, such as free help lines (see Appendix 1).

Dermot Flynn, Team Manager for the drug and alcohol service at state-funded mental health provider South Essex Partnership Trust (SEPT), points out that at this stage friends and family often can't do much more than provide the problem drinker with information on safe drinking guidelines. They can try to sit down with them in a non-confrontational way, but this should not be when they are intoxicated as this increases the potential for conflict. If the drinker simply sees the information, this may be the key that gets them to consider it in time.

'Anybody who the individual would be prepared to talk to could in theory help,' says Flynn, 'and they might just manage to get the drinker starting to think. But often it is the occurrence of a stressful or life event that causes change and makes them realize they've been overdoing it. For example, a drink-driving conviction or concerns expressed by social services about their ability to look after their children can be especially good at focusing their concentration. Following discussion with their GP, there may be evidence that damage to their liver has occurred due to their alcohol intake and this can give them the impetus to cut down their alcohol use.'

Strike When the Iron is Hot

Things tend to get much easier for friends and family who want to help once a drinker reaches the 'contemplation stage' and considers the possibility that alcohol could be a problem and that they need to do something about it. This is the best stage at which you can help someone, and if you weren't able to successfully bring sources of help to their attention at the pre-contemplation stage, you may be successful if you try again now.

Now is the ideal time to get them to consider phoning an EAP or other relevant helpline, to seek advice from their GP or, if they have one, their occupational health department at work. You might also wish to introduce them to online services that can help people cut down on drinking, such as Moderation Management (www.moderation.org) or www.lookatyourdrinking.com (See pages 223 to 224).

Another way of helping them is recommending that they write a drink diary to monitor exactly what and how much they are drinking, when and where they are drinking it, with whom they are drinking it and how they feel both before and after their drinking sessions. This should help them identify the triggers that make them drink and drink to excess.

'Are you lucky enough to have a trusted, kind friend willing to listen to you blow off steam about breaking a drinking habit? Or a buddy who is also practicing the program and shooting for a safe drinking goal? If so, take advantage of the relationship. Call him up at the time you'd normally settle into your drinking routine. Discuss your feelings about drinking. Or the latest news. Invite him to dinner or a movie. Anything – as long as it keeps you from engaging in that old problem-drinking pattern.'

Donna J. Cornett from *7 Weeks to Safe Social Drinking*

Pointing them in the direction of some of the better quality de-alcoholized and alcohol-free beers and wines that have become available in recent years could also prove valuable. There are some potentially good reasons why those seeking to go completely dry should be wary of alcohol substitutes, but they can be useful for those intent on cutting down, or for pregnant women and others who are seeking only to give up for an initial period. Some of the newer substitute wines taste so realistic that they have even won international awards in blind taste tests against wines containing alcohol.

Some of the more realistic substitutes are produced in the same way as their standard counterparts, right up until the bottling takes place, at which point the alcohol is removed.

This means that the flavour and other original characteristics remain, including the anti-oxidants that can provide health benefits to moderate drinkers. It also means that these drinks contain markedly fewer calories than standard wines and beers, which has obvious advantages to those who are keeping an eye on their weight.

'At the contemplation stage they start to want to explore the potential benefits of drinking less,' explains SEPT's Dermot Flynn. 'They might, for example, start becoming open to the idea that cutting down may result in them having more money, enable them to drop the kids off at school, and improve their health, appearance and dietary intake. This is the stage at which to challenge the positive beliefs that an individual might have about alcohol.'

Flynn points out that people often think alcohol helps with stress and that it makes them more sociable, but you can discuss the fact that the stress will still be there the next morning. You can also gently point out that once they've had a few too many they might not be the life and soul of the party, as they think they are. Alcohol might make them overbearing and they probably don't realize that people are stepping back from them.

> 'Normally inhibited people don't become more interesting when they are inebriated; on the contrary, they become overemotional, repetitive, incoherent and boring. It wouldn't be so bad if the inhibited person felt better for it, but they don't; they are in a stupor and you cannot appreciate a situation unless you have your senses to appreciate it with.'
>
> Allen Carr from *The Easy Way to Stop Drinking*

At this contemplation stage it's important to give the drinker as much encouragement as possible, after all, the more people they have support from the better. It's worth mentioning at this stage that from now on you must endeavour to do the bulk of your own drinking outside the home. This will reinforce the fact that you are on their side and reduces the chances of them being tempted. If they come across a beer in the fridge it might make it that bit more difficult to say no.

Peter Smith at Broadway Lodge says, 'If *you* change then there is a likelihood that *they* will change, so why not stop drinking at home and go out with your mates. If you enjoy a drink and have no problems with alcohol, then there is no reason why you should stop drinking, but if a person is thinking of cutting down or has already done so, then it's only fair to support them in the early stages. If you drink at home it also becomes more difficult to challenge the drinker.'

Continuing Support

This support must obviously continue when a drinker has decided what plan of action to take to control their drinking. You should encourage and support them throughout its implementation and say what a good idea you think it is, but also realize that it must be them, not you, who introduces the plan. At this stage, most drinkers will ask for some support and assistance from partners or close family, and some may seek assistance from further afield.

Your support should continue even if the drinker slips up and departs from their plan in response to a specific setback, such as having a row with their boss. This is known as a 'lapse' as opposed to a 'relapse', which involves reverting to their previous levels of drinking for a sustained period. Your approach should be to discuss the reasonableness of their response to the situation in question and to help them work out how they are going to deal with a similar situation next time. Try and stress that a lapse is only a lapse and that it should prove useful as they'll learn from it.

'When people set out to make any significant change, it's common to have some setbacks. What we've seen after treatment is that as people reduce their use, their episodes of overdoing it get farther apart and happen less often, and they also drink far less on days when they do drink. Most reduce their alcohol use by well more than half, drinking less often and much less per occasion.'

William R. Miller and Ricardo F. Munoz from
Controlling Your Drinking

Always try to offer positive encouragement and highlight the benefits of what they have achieved – for example, the fact that they are less grumpy or able to spend more time with their kids. Such feedback can give them a strong basis for wanting to continue. Indeed, because family members and close friends will know the drinker's general persona, they can be of more use than a counsellor in terms of offering the right kind of support and knowing when to jump in. You can, for example, congratulate them on turning down a drink at a party and saying what a great evening it's been. You can also help them avoid high-risk situations by liaising – at the drinker's request and on their behalf – with family and friends holding functions. When approached in the right way, a bride and groom may be quite understanding as to why someone trying to cut down their drinking might be able to attend the actual wedding service but not the reception – although it's preferable for the drinker to make such 'apologies' for themselves.

Cultural considerations can also come into play here, because in some countries, such as Scotland and Ireland, it's far less acceptable to be sober at a wedding or funeral than in England. Even in England the drinking culture is likely to be more difficult to handle for someone trying to cut down than is the case in the US, simply because drinking is more ingrained in British society.

▨ CASE STUDIES Local Culture Can Make a Huge Difference

As we can see from the two case studies below, attitudes towards drinking vary markedly between one country and another, and this can be a significant factor for someone trying to cut down. Both subjects are middle-aged female PR executives who decided to try to reduce their alcohol intake as a result of suffering from breast cancer. The heavy drinking culture in the UK clearly made this harder to achieve for one than for the other who, following a move to the US, found herself in far more abstemious surroundings.

One thing that clearly crosses all geographical boundaries, however, is the benefit of having a supportive partner when seeking to cut back on the booze.

Temptation All Around

When fifty-three-year-old Londoner Sarah Cooper had finished her treatment for breast cancer in May 2009, sobriety suddenly became an urgent priority. She had read a book written by one of the consultants at the breast cancer prevention centre she'd attended, and it explained that every alcoholic drink she consumed would significantly increase the chances of her breast cancer recurring.

Finding the information 'scary', she vowed to stop drinking completely during the week and to only allow herself four large glasses of wine in total at the weekend, which would keep her just within the UK government's weekly safe drinking guidelines for women.

'My partner has been very supportive of me, encouraging me and regularly congratulating me whenever I triumphantly announced, "Three days without booze".'

'I probably drank half a bottle of red wine every day before my illness,' Sarah says, 'plus lots more every weekend. Dinner simply wasn't dinner without a nice glass of Rioja! I wasn't drinking to get drunk, but just because I loved wine – and the fact that it helped to take the edge off a stressful day was an added bonus. I couldn't believe how quickly I got to within the limit I set myself, or how difficult it was to stop drinking during the week.

'At home I would seethe silently as my partner poured himself a glass of red. I've now bought myself a very nice set of teas, although originally I bought low-alcohol wine and poured it into a wine glass to recreate the experience. But it was only grape juice, so who was I kidding? Having said that, my partner has been very supportive of me, encouraging me and regularly congratulating me whenever I triumphantly announced, "Three days without booze". The fact that alcohol often makes him depressed has meant that he has now joined me in our enforced abstinence during the week, which definitely helps.'

Outside the home the task has proved far more difficult, and it didn't take her long to realize that British culture is centred on drinking. During the first week of her new regime, a charity fundraising event she attended on Saturday centred on fizz; a jazz recital in a church on Tuesday night had wine on offer at the interval, and everyone at a quiz night on the Wednesday seemed to be drunk.

> 'The most difficult thing is trying to control my drinking with my more hedonistic companions at the weekend.'

'Gluttony loves company,' Sarah continues, 'and no one wants a sober member of the party remembering all the crazy stuff that goes on. People certainly don't force me to drink, and nobody would comment if I had water instead of wine, but the very fact that they are all drinking is the most difficult thing. I try to socialize with my all-too-few non-drinking friends during the week now, but the most difficult thing is trying to control my drinking with my more hedonistic companions at the weekend.

'On a night out at the weekend everyone tops up glasses with abandon. I could, of course, announce that I am only drinking two glasses of wine that evening, but everyone gets drunk and forgets. Blaming other people for your own drinking habits seems completely lame, however, and I know there are plenty of steps I could take, such as alternating water with wine, drinking more slowly, drinking spritzers, or just saying, "No thanks." I start each evening with such good intentions, but I still occasionally wake up reaching for the aspirin and the sackcloth to pay penance!'

US Culture Helps Cutting Down

Having worked in PR in London, fifty-eight-year-old Jo Scholes moved to Los Angeles five years ago. She was a binge drinker during the early stages of her career, although she started to cut down her alcohol intake in her forties to ensure her performance at work didn't suffer. After being diagnosed with breast cancer at the age of fifty-one, however, she has cut right down to one or two alcoholic drinks a week – usually red wine.

'The only time I drink more is when I visit the UK,' she says. 'Drinking has become a naughty treat now and frankly I enjoy it more, but I have to discipline myself not to have another. There is no social pressure to drink in the US, but in some places there is social pressure not to drink. Remember, this is a country where there was prohibition and people need their cars here more. Public transport is patchy and you can't fall into a cab at the end of the evening. If a couple are seen having a bottle of wine there is often an assumption that it is a special occasion.'

> 'There is no doubt that much alcohol consumption is down to habit and, because my life has changed, I now spend time with people who have different habits.'

A middle-class person going out to drink here might have one glass of wine, whereas in England one was always having half a bottle. Occasionally I feel a bit out of place when I decide to have a second drink, which is a bit of a role reversal from my final years in the UK PR industry, when I tended to be the relatively sober one amongst a crowd of binge drinkers. I have an acquaintance in the US who's whispered to have a bit of a problem because she invariably orders a single glass of red wine with meals, and when we were invited to a picnic on the beach recently the host got terribly twitchy about someone downing a couple of cans of beer!'

Jo, who has been vegetarian for twenty years, finds that during her visits to the UK her heavier-drinking friends are more likely to comment on her vegetarianism than on her abstinence from alcohol. They can, however, still influence her ability to drink a little.

> 'If your spouse drinks you tend to end up sharing a bottle of wine because it's better value than buying it by the glass, so you end up drinking more.'

'There is no doubt that much alcohol consumption is down to habit and, because my life has changed, I now spend time with people who have different habits. The fact that my partner has recently stopped drinking altogether as part of a health drive has also undoubtedly made it easier for me to drink less. When a couple both drink there is an assumption that when you go out for a meal or to a bar you will be drinking. The question is what you will have rather than whether you would like a drink.

'If your spouse drinks you tend to end up sharing a bottle of wine because it's better value than buying it by the glass, so you end up drinking more. But when I have a drink nowadays I do so because I've made a conscious decision, and maybe that's why I enjoy every drop of the odd glass of wine, the occasional Martini and the rare Scotch. On my birthday I will have a glass of Scotch and it will be special.'

Dealing With Relapse

If lapses are becoming frequent and the plan they are sticking to doesn't seem to be working, there is a lot to be said for encouraging a drinker who wants to cut back to consider alternative plans or an entirely new approach. Some methods work for some but not for others and, as with trying to find the best way to help more seriously addicted drinkers, there is a certain amount of trial and error involved.

If, however, the drinker has a complete relapse and reverts to their previous levels of drinking, it may be time to suggest they stop drinking altogether for a period, in order to examine the underlying problems causing their unhealthy relationship with alcohol and to get their life sorted out. If you are lucky they might then appreciate the benefits of sobriety so much they decide not to go back to drinking again, but if they repeatedly relapse you should start considering some of the methods described in Chapter 4 for encouraging them to seek professional help.

'Addiction is a relapsing condition,' continues Addaction's Julie Breslin, 'and you need to be wary of the fact that someone might just be saying they keep lapsing when they have in fact reverted to previous problem behaviour. If someone goes to a family wedding and wakes up with a king-sized hangover, but shows plenty of remorse and immediately goes back to following their plan, there shouldn't be too much to worry about. But if someone is repeatedly starting to think of alcohol, you might well have a relapse situation.'

Breslin points out that if they have clearly had a relapse it may be worth hinting that they have lost control and should consider giving up for an initial period. In many cases the idea of not being able to drink for the rest of their lives can be too much to take and can make a drinker less likely to cooperate. But, she explains, even though someone with a serious addiction is unlikely to successfully return to drinking in moderation, just the fact that they are drinking less for brief periods is a positive sign. Not only will they give their liver a rest, they'll reduce the chances of falls and injuries and of getting into dangerous situations.

Not For Everyone

The simple fact of the matter is that cutting down won't work for everybody. For some it can be harder than quitting, but for others it can be easier, and the drinker has to decide what works best for them. William R. Miller and Ricardo F. Munoz, authors of *Controlling Your Drinking*, are extremely up front about the fact that not all those who follow their methods will be successful.

They report that their research following participants over periods of three to eight years after they had completed the programme showed that in the twelve months prior to the follow-up only one in seven had maintained complete moderation throughout the year, which is defined as staying under three drinks per day and averaging ten standard drinks per week without any alcohol-related problems or signs of alcohol dependence. Another 23 per cent had reduced their drinking substantially, while a further 24 per cent had been totally abstinent for at least a year. This left 37 per cent continuing with heavy, harmful drinking.

Dr David Bremner, Medical Director of Dutch online addiction treatment provider Tactus International, says, 'Several studies have shown that the chances of successfully remaining a moderate drinker are greater if you are under forty, there is no history of alcoholism in your family, you aren't having or haven't previously had withdrawal symptoms, you are female, have had a problem with drinking for less than ten years, you don't have problems in other areas of life and you've been a moderate drinker before.'

Significantly, both lookatyourdrinking.com and Moderation Management, which offer worldwide Internet-based services for those seeking to reduce the amount they drink, place great emphasis on the fact that cutting down is not a viable solution for everyone, and offer abstinence programmes as alternatives.

Lookatyourdrinking.com

Online addiction programme lookatyourdrinking.com, which, as its name suggests, can be accessed worldwide on www. lookatyourdrinking.com, is currently available in English, Dutch and German. It has been created by a team of leading psychiatrists, psychologists and online treatment specialists from Tactus International, one of Holland's largest treatment centres, and consists of five constituent parts: information, online contact, e-therapy, aftercare and scientific research.

The online contact enables people concerned about their drinking habits to exchange experiences and receive support from others in similar situations, while the e-therapy component uses accredited therapists in an online environment and can be accessed anonymously, if the client wishes. The latter offers an option to cut down or quit alcohol altogether, and a personal therapist works with the client via the Internet to find the right solution. A course of treatment normally lasts twelve to sixteen weeks.

The client will see a picture of their therapist and know their name, but the communication between client and therapist is fully online/web-based through a secure inbox on the website. The therapist, who uses a combination of cognitive behavioural therapy (CBT) and motivational interviewing (MI), always replies within three working days.

The client sets their own goals with the help of their therapist and is assigned a series of exercises, work assignments or homework. Using an innovative and interactive piece of easy-to-use software, they are also encouraged to keep an alcohol logbook to explain when, why and how they drink. This can help them to gain more insight into their drinking patterns.

■ CASE STUDIES Cutting Down Online Produces Very Different Solutions

As demonstrated by these two first-hand accounts from users of lookatyourdrinking.com, different people have very different views about what level of drinking constitutes a problem and what the best potential solution should be.

Drinking Less Than a Third of What He Used to

Mark Goater, a forty-five-year-old businessman who lives in Nottingham, still keeps an alcohol diary despite finishing the lookatyourdrinking.com programme several weeks ago. He uses it to record any situations that he finds difficult as well as things that have gone well for him. 'I've had some difficult things to deal with in both my personal and working life,' Mark explains, 'but instead of heading for the pub when things get on top of me, now I'll have a soft drink or a glass of water. Keeping an alcohol diary has brought it home to me that I'm responsible for my actions.'

Before approaching lookatyourdrinking.com, Mark, who is married with two children, drank very slightly less than the weekly limits the UK Government sets out as being sensible for men, which is around three times less than the average user of the service and under five times less than some of the heaviest drinking users. Nevertheless, he still felt he had a problem he needed to deal with, especially as his job involved a lot of driving.

'I now drink simply because I like the taste and not because I tell myself I've earned a reward.'

'Drinking had ceased to be a social pastime for me,' he explains. 'I was drinking to change the way I felt, especially if I felt uncomfortable or awkward in social situations. When I got home from work at around six in the evening I always felt very tired and had three or four small cans of beer straight away. The other members of my family never commented on it, but deep down I knew that wasn't normal behaviour.

'I wasn't going to work with hangovers, but alcohol was playing an important part in my life and I no longer had control of my drinking. My wife likes a drink, but she knows when she's had enough. I, on the other hand, have been really stupid in the past and have driven over the drink-driving limit on several occasions. A couple of times I've been completely drunk and could have killed myself or, worse, someone else.'

Working with his therapist from the e-therapy module of lookatyourdrinking.com, Mark decided to cut his consumption of twenty half pints of beer a week down to a maximum of six, and he found the cutting-down process much easier than he'd originally anticipated.

'I discovered that I can have and enjoy just one drink in isolation,' he continues. 'I now drink simply because I like the taste and not because I tell myself I've earned a reward. I would like to stick to this way of drinking, although I have to admit to being a bit worried about Christmas. I'm not ruling out the possibility that things might slip, but I think that I have now learned enough to know what to do if that happens.'

Quitting Turns Out to Be the Best Solution

Hindsight can be a wonderful thing and fifty-five-year-old Felicity Dixon now realizes that she had in fact had a drink problem from the age of twenty right up until signing up with lookatyourdrinking.com a year ago. She had never talked to her GP about the issue and had always kidded herself that she was only a social drinker, but every time she came up against a problem she found she couldn't cope without turning to drink.

When her twenty-five-year relationship with her partner came to an end eighteen months ago her drinking accelerated to a whole new level. Felicity, who works in advertising, could not get through the day without drinking a bottle of wine and often topped this up in the evening with several vodkas and tonics.

'I always told myself that it wasn't that bad and that I could sort it out myself, but the reality was that I was drinking to avoid dealing with my problems,' she explains. 'I had lost all control and my health was clearly beginning to suffer. It was only when I read an article about lookatyourdrinking.com in the press about a year ago that the denial came to an end.'

Signing up straight away, she began working with her e-therapist and, by the time she had completed the course three months later, she had decided that giving up altogether was the best solution for her. Homework assignments had included keeping a daily log of how much she drank and looking at the triggers that led her to start drinking.

> 'I always told myself that it wasn't that bad and that I could sort it out myself but the reality was that I was drinking to avoid dealing with my problems.'

'It's still quite hard for me, but now I've stopped drinking completely,' she explains. 'The most important thing for me was that the treatment was individually tailored and that I could do my homework in my own time. My therapist listened and understood exactly what I was saying, and focused on the real issues. The whole programme and approach was methodical and easy to work through.

'There was no attempt to dig around in my past, but I was given practical tips that helped me address what I was going through. I discovered patterns to my drinking which I hadn't recognized before and I was able to look at my reasons for wanting to drink, and examine what I thought I was getting from drinking. That gave me the opportunity to look at how I could deal with things differently and find other ways of coping with my day-to-day issues.

'Stopping drinking wasn't that difficult, but I've managed to stay stopped, which had always been my problem in the past,' she continues. 'I have learned that I need to stop and think whenever I feel like a drink. I know now that a drink is only going to make things worse, never better.'

Moderation Management

Moderation Management (MM) is a behavioural change programme and national support group network for people who want to reduce their drinking to non-harmful levels. It also encourages other positive lifestyle changes. An underlying assumption is that each person accepts personal responsibility for choosing and maintaining their own path, whether that's moderation or abstinence. It can be accessed in English worldwide on www.moderation.org and also offers the chance to participate in free face-to-face meetings in eighteen US states, as well as in Canada, Australia, Ireland, Thailand and the UK.

The nine-step professionally reviewed programme provides information about alcohol, moderate drinking guidelines and limits, drink monitoring exercises, goal-setting techniques and self-management strategies. It can also be used to find balance and moderation in many other areas of drinkers' lives, one small step at a time. It attracts largely well-educated middle-class people who are mildly to moderately alcohol dependent, and about 30 per cent of members go on to abstinence-based programmes.

Moderation programmes shorten the process of discovering whether or not moderation is a workable solution by providing concrete guidelines about the limits of moderate alcohol consumption, as well as various behavioural techniques to reduce both the amount that's drunk and the frequency. After completing thirty days of abstinence and attempting behavioural change techniques, some drinkers may discover that moderation is too difficult or just not worth the trouble. At that point many choose the path of abstinence. Some members who choose abstinence remain in the MM programme in a separate online group for 'Absers', while others find an abstinence-only programme to attend.

'I enjoy bananas, but if I overindulged in them and woke the following morning with a throbbing head and a sudden need to be sick, I wouldn't repeat the exercise the very same day. If bananas caused me half the problems alcohol did, I'd never go near another banana in my life.'

Allen Carr from *No More Hangovers*

Dr Ana Kosok, executive director of MM, says, 'Traditional approaches based on the disease model and concept of powerlessness can be counter-productive for some people, particularly women and minorities. But the MM approach doesn't work for everyone and, when it doesn't work, abstinence may be more appropriate.'

She warns that the family of any problem drinker is understandably terrified that controlled drinking won't work, so the person who learns to drink moderately must regain the family's trust by demonstrating their responsible behaviour over time. Those who have been pushed to attend by their family or employer may feel quite rebellious, so one of the first things MM does is to encourage separation from the family's demands. This enables the drinker to distinguish their own desire to change from others' pressure and judgement.

Dr Kosok also emphasizes that a strong personal motivation is needed to make these difficult changes and that each person's motivation is different. It may be health, appearance, reputation, fear of hurting others while drinking, or any one of many things.

'Motivation is key,' she continues, 'and an important motivation can be preserving a valued relationship. A relationship can be really powerful and I've seen people make incredible changes in cutting down drinking for the benefit of a partner or family. Another way to clarify motivation is to elicit their most closely held values and ask whether their drinking runs counter to these. Examples might be wanting to be a good example for their children or a respected member of the community.'

Dr Kosok stresses that in a marriage there may be two problems: the drinker's drinking and the spouse's perception of it. A wife, for example, may have had a father who abused alcohol. For her, even if her spouse successfully moderates his drinking to non-harmful levels, any drinking at all may trigger fears rooted in her past. Here, communication and negotiation are key.

Such a couple would need to discuss his drinking in terms of magnitude and harm and in terms of her personal fears. How much drinking will she consider reasonable? For example, he might like four drinks during an evening, while she would like no more than one herself. Perhaps they could agree on a compromise of no more than three drinks ever, no more than three drinking nights a week and no Martinis ever. Limits must be established and adhered to.

'Communication about much more than the number of drinks per night is needed,' explains Dr Kosok. 'MM's broad framework and members' shared experiences provide the basis for this kind of communication. Drinking can often mask other issues in a marriage, typically power issues. MM understands problem drinking as a behaviour occurring along a continuum, with many contributing factors. In this context, being labelled the family alcoholic is part of a larger issue, with implications of who has the most power, who is "good", who is "bad" and who is to blame for any and all problems.'

Dr Kosok points out that it can be really helpful if the significant other also refrains from drinking during an initial thirty-day abstinence period, makes a point of not bringing alcohol home when their partner is making the effort to cut back and voices support. But she adds that it's just as important not to act as a policeman and count drinks.

▨ CASE STUDY Family Feedback Proves Crucial

When forty-two-year-old Paul Collins used to work in a highly pressurized IT role, having a glass of wine the moment he returned home had become as automatic as taking his coat off. He didn't even have to open a bottle because his fifty-four-year-old wife Anne would normally have started her second glass by the time he arrived.

Like most of her friends, Anne would typically down two or three large glasses of wine a night and Paul frequently had even more than that. Additionally, on a Saturday or Sunday it was not unusual for the couple to drink an entire bottle each. But neither they nor anyone they knew considered their alcohol consumption to be in any way excessive.

Nevertheless, attitudes towards alcohol in the Collins household changed markedly in early 2008, soon after Anne saw an advert asking for 'normal mums who probably drink a little more wine than they should' to take part in a TV documentary. And it wasn't just Paul who felt the repercussions. All their three children, eighteen-year-old Aaron, fifteen-year-old Brooke and thirteen-year-old Euan, found themselves with pivotal roles.

'The positive feedback that she constantly got from her husband and kids made all the difference.'

Armed with camcorders, the youngsters were required to film their mother every time she went to the fridge, opened a wine bottle or topped up her glass. They even filmed her taking out her recycling crate full of two weeks' worth of empty bottles.

All three also appeared in the documentary, travelling with Anne to see a liver specialist to find out the results of the liver test she had undergone a week earlier. This certainly had the effect of making Anne realize that drinking was a serious matter. Fortunately, the results weren't too alarming, but the specialist advised that it would be 'extraordinarily beneficial to her health' to cut down, especially as she had stomach problems. He also recommended that, initially, she give up altogether for a month.

As soon as he heard the news, Paul volunteered that he would also quit drinking for that first month to show support, and Anne admits that this made her task very much easier. Additionally, the positive feedback she constantly got from her husband and kids made all the difference.

Anne, who runs her own business organizing children's parties, cookery and after-school clubs, says, 'The cooperation of your family is very important and the first step is to clear out all the alcohol from the house with their support. During my month of going dry we didn't drink at home at all, but after that it didn't matter quite so much that Paul went back to drinking regularly. During the first few days I thought I was going to struggle as it felt like the very early stages of a diet when you think you've lost weight but haven't. It was really important to be told how well I looked so I knew I wasn't imagining it.

'It also really encouraged me when the children mentioned what a difference it made now that I was able to give them lifts to places and wasn't always forgetting favours I'd promised them when I'd been drinking. Praise is the most natural commodity you need when you are trying to battle the bottle and, although Paul is not a natural praiser, he soon cottoned on. All my family have been terribly supportive and they have become ingrained in my new habit.'

'Praise is the most natural commodity you need when you are trying to battle the bottle.'

Anne now sticks rigidly to the UK Government's safe drinking guidelines, never drinking more than four large glasses of wine in an entire week and limiting her drinking almost exclusively to weekends. This means she drinks about a quarter of what she used to. Her task has been made easier by the fact that Paul, who now runs his own gardening maintenance business, stopped drinking alcohol altogether four months ago.

'To make cutting down work you must have at least two or three alcohol-free nights a week and Paul couldn't manage it, so he quit,' she continues. 'It's very helpful that he doesn't drink, and I would never now intentionally get tipsy as I wouldn't want to look stupid in front of him. I'm also very proud of the fact that none of my kids has seen me drunk. Brooke sometimes mischievously tries to egg me on to see how I would behave if I got tipsy, but she knows I won't do it.'

In summary

- It is important to realize that cutting down won't work for someone with a physical addiction and that, whilst it can work for some drinkers with psychological addictions, it doesn't for others

- If someone is trying to cut down you may be able to do a lot to help and the 'contemplation stage' provides the best opportunity to do this

- In some cases simply being willing to listen or gently nudging a work colleague in the direction of the EAP (Employee Assistance Programme) may be all that is required

- Provide ongoing encouragement and highlight the benefits of what they've achieved and, if the drinker slips up temporarily, stress that a lapse is only a lapse and can be a useful learning curve

CHAPTER FOUR

Dealing with a Seriously Addicted Drinker

S ome of the principles involved in dealing with a seriously addicted drinker are the same as those outlined in Chapter 3 for helping someone cut down. In particular, the decision to do something about the drink problem must come from the drinker themselves and not from those around them. Friends and family members should also avoid discussing their drinking with them when they are drunk, and should try to be as encouraging and helpful as possible and to draw on all possible reserves of patience, because the recovery process can be a long and drawn-out one.

In those cases where drinkers with physical addictions or the worst kind of psychological addictions are willing to admit they have a problem, the considerations are broadly similar to those outlined in 'The contemplation stage' in Chapter 3. The big difference is that you should probably be looking to refer to more specialist forms of help.

Dr Niall Campbell from The Priory Hospital says, 'Are they recognizing that they have a problem? If so, get them to seek medical help from an addiction specialist, as opposed to a GP. They might decide that there are appropriate medications that can be prescribed and may feel they have an additional depressive illness that needs treating.'

In practice, however, many of those with more serious forms of addiction are in denial, and this is why you are likely to be playing a whole different ball game. Unlike many of those drinkers cutting down, they haven't volunteered that they have an unhealthy relationship with alcohol or asked for your help in combating it. If, therefore, you behave in a way that could be construed as advising or lecturing them, it could have exactly the opposite effect to the one intended by making them angry and resulting in them drinking more.

'Denial is a defense mechanism, a natural response to protect against pain. When someone feels helpless to impact their situation or is ashamed of what is occurring, they often resort to denial. Denial can be identified when individuals discount, minimize, or rationalize their feelings.'

Claudia Black from *Changing Course*

Actions can wind up drinkers just as easily as words. For example, if you have agreed to help someone cut down or give up for a brief period they are likely to really appreciate it if you invite them round to your place for a meal when no alcohol is present. If, on the other hand, the drinker is in denial, such a gesture could really backfire. The key message to take on board is that, should you decide not to drink in front of them, it's important to do so in a way that doesn't seem patronizing. The idea is to set a subtle example rather than appear judgemental.

Bearing this in mind, alcohol experts can express markedly different views on whether friends and loved ones should in fact be drinking alcohol in front of those with drink problems or indeed drinking alcohol at all, even if it is away from the home with their friends. Advice on dealing with a problem drinker often focuses heavily on *not* changing your own behaviour, because this helps them to take personal responsibility for their actions and makes them conclude there is no one else to blame for their drink problem but themselves.

Dr Bruce Trathen, Consultant Addiction Psychiatrist at dry-outnow.com, says, 'I think there is something in the idea that a person with a problem who has decided to do something about it should ideally be supported in creating "safe havens of non-drinking environments", and this is usually the home. Such an ideal is often unattainable, but if it is attainable then it is for the best, as individuals with more effective social support have better progress.

'But as a relative or friend, I think you should only do what you feel like doing, otherwise you are potentially creating an artificial environment you might not feel like supporting in the longer term. The basic message is that it's still down to the individual with the problem to find a way to remain dry, whatever the surrounding environment threatens.'

Professor Cary Cooper from Lancaster University Management School, says, 'If you are a spouse, friend or partner of a problem drinker, then I don't think you should be drinking at all, full stop. Just think about what you are saying to them if you do. The most powerful way of influencing people is by your own behaviour.

'Be receptive and listen. Let them know you care about them and be there as an open conduit for their emotions but don't confront them, and they might come to their own conclusions that they need help. The more patronizing you are and the more you push it down their throat, the less likely you are to succeed. Also, be emotionally literate and share problems you have with others, particularly with the drinker, because they tend to make assumptions that they are the only ones with problems, so it can be good to show you are vulnerable.

'Even if you've tried everything else and failed, you need to make sure you are a good role model and maintain your own health,' he continues. 'You should have a better lifestyle which should extend beyond not drinking and should include taking exercise. But don't say anything about the fact that you are not drinking or brag about it. Just do it, and if they ask you about it just say that you prefer to be healthy.'

▨ CASE STUDY Daughter's Messages Make All the Difference in Rehab

Tessa Salter's attempts to hide her drinking from her teenage daughter Sally-Anne were none too successful. She used to fill orange juice cartons with wine, leaving an inch or two of the juice so the mixture still looked orange. Sally-Anne would ask if she could have a sip and her mother would make a big fuss about the fact that she couldn't, implying that it was a ridiculous thing to ask. Deep down they both knew what was going on.

In 1999 Tessa, who is now forty-eight, turned to drink after the recruitment company she had set up lost a lucrative contract to a rival. Despite checking herself into The Priory Hospital in Chelmsford, she found she wasn't able to consider giving up drinking when the counsellors there suggested she went on an abstinence programme, so after only a couple of weeks she signed herself out.

> 'She simply couldn't face up to how bad her problem had become, and she ignored her GP's advice to attend AA.'

Twelve months later her ten-year marriage to childhood sweetheart Martin buckled under the strain of her drinking, but even this didn't provide sufficient incentive for her to stop. Despite having to make several visits to casualty after cracking her head open when falling or slipping in the shower, she simply couldn't face up to how bad her problem had become, and she ignored her GP's advice to attend AA. At her most reckless, she even drove Sally-Anne and her younger brother Tim to school whilst well over the drink-drive limit.

Even after getting back together with Martin, her life continued to spiral out of control and, having become increasingly paranoid that the police were on to her drink driving, by 2006 she frequently found herself unable to get up and see the children off to school. That April she reached her lowest ebb and, after she had cut her wrists, Martin rushed her to hospital. Believing she would die if she didn't get proper help, he then drove her to The Priory for a second attempt at rehab.

Tessa is in no doubt as to what constituted the single most important factor in ensuring that her twenty-eight-day stay in rehab was successful and that she has remained dry ever since. When she unpacked her bags on the first night she found twenty-eight envelopes, each one containing a supportive note from Sally-Anne. Every night she would open a new one and it would tell her just how much her sixteen-year-old daughter loved her.

'For her to do something as touching as that made a huge contribution towards making me feel well and making me realize how much was at stake.'

Tessa, who is now training to be an addiction counsellor, says, 'The notes really spurred me on to take control of my life. She hadn't been pleasant to me for ages and my drinking certainly hadn't helped in that respect. I wasn't there for her and she had been punishing me for a long time, so for her to do something as touching as that made a huge contribution towards making me feel well and making me realize how much was at stake. Lines of communication are everything and, although tough love can be quite powerful, it doesn't work in all cases.'

Tessa is still married to Martin, who also stopped drinking two years ago at the age of fifty-four. She hasn't experienced any cravings and, although she occasionally finds the odd bout of self-pity sets in, this has never been serious enough to trigger a return to drinking. Attending AA twice a week since leaving The Priory has played an important part in her recovery.

Looking After Number One

Remember that your own health and state of mind is crucial in this process, too. Right from the beginning your focus should be on securing your own mental wellbeing and happiness as well as your physical health by using some of the methods described in Chapter 7. This is not something that should be confined to the 'too difficult pile' until you decide there is literally nothing left you can do to help the drinker. It should be a very high priority from day one. Apart from anything else, taking due care of yourself should ultimately help the drinker.

Don Lavender from Camino Recovery says, 'It is of immense value for the family or friends of those with drink problems to look at their own issues as opposed to the problems of the drinker. The best way for the family and friends to help the drinker is to get help for themselves.'

'The message to the family member or friend of the alcoholic is: "You are paying a tremendous price for living with alcoholism, and you may be contributing to your alcoholic's drinking. You don't have to live the way you are living. Seek help for yourself. A change in your attitudes and behaviour will ultimately affect the alcoholic, who then may seek help."'

Gordon MacRae, from the foreword to *The Courage to Change*

The simple fact of the matter is that whether or not you have yet reached a stage that would meet official definitions of being co-dependent, the strains and stresses of dealing with the drinker will be negatively affecting you. Furthermore, the harder you try to help the drinker come to the realization that they need professional help, the more stressful it is likely to become.

Nick Barton, Chief Executive of national charity Action on Addiction, says, 'Right from the beginning make sure you look after yourself. Don't get consumed by the other person, but that doesn't mean being completely neglectful of them. Provide core empathy and support but avoid desperately trying to control the person out of your own need. People with drink problems pick up on things and know where you are coming from.'

At all times remember that you have done nothing wrong. You did not cause the drinking and you cannot actually stop the drinking yourself. You are merely living with the consequences of the drinking, although you are unusually well placed to act as part of a support mechanism to help the drinker come to the realization that they have a problem.

Just as we compared finding the correct treatment method to having a bunch of keys and needing to find the right key to fit the drinker's door (see Chapter 1, page 7), one could compare the task of trying to get the drinker to acknowledge that they need help to needing another slightly different set of keys.

Later in this chapter we detail some of the more formalized methods that can be tried to communicate with a drinker if the natural relationship approach fails to work, and it may be that one method has to be tried after another.

Whether you are trying the formalized methods or natural relationship-type approaches referred to above, it is important to realize that meeting with at least some kind of resistance is inevitable when you are still at the stage of trying to proactively help. Skilful use of words and actions on your part can, however, help minimize the extent of this resistance.

'When confronted with another's unjust anger, silently refuse to accept it. Smile inwardly and say to yourself, "I hear the words, but they don't speak about my real self. I refuse to treat this anger as justified. Since I don't deserve this anger, I need not validate it by an angry response.'

Evelyn Leite from Detachment

Particularly Stressful Situations

It is not uncommon for those with serious drink problems to express suicidal thoughts, and this can be an extremely disturbing experience for those closest to them. There are undoubtedly many cases when the drinker does this simply to justify their drinking, but even this can be viewed as a less direct desire to kill themselves.

Professor Roger Williams, Director of the Institute of Hepatology, London, International Centre for Research into Liver Disorders, says, 'Some alcoholics will never stop drinking and will carry on doing this until they die. In some cases there is no way they are going to stop because, in their view, they have nothing left to live for. There is a very strong association between suicide and alcoholism, and if the person expressing the wish has a reasonable background then you have to bring in every possible support you can get, including the family, the GP and, if possible, a psychiatrist. The evidence is that some 40 to 50 per cent of alcoholics that have developed cirrhosis will stop drinking when they learn of the damage to their liver and likely survival outcome.'

The majority of alcohol experts stress that the link between alcohol and suicide is so strong that you cannot afford to risk not taking someone seriously when they express suicidal thoughts. Once suicidal thoughts come into play it starts becoming a mental health issue rather than one of addiction, so family and friends should urgently contact local mental health services.

In countries such as the UK, where mental health legislation does not permit someone to be confined simply as a result of problem drinking, such a situation can be a welcome opportunity to bring things to a head and break the pattern of denial.

By undergoing emergency psychiatric help and possibly being

referred for residential rehab or other treatment, the drinker may at last start to show awareness of the fact that they have a drink problem and be prepared to discuss potential solutions to it with those around them.

Consultant Physician Professor John Saunders of the University of Sydney, Australia, says, 'A person voicing suicidal ideas is at risk of suicide, and completed suicide is fifteen to twenty times more likely in alcohol-dependent people than it is in the general population. I would take statements that they want to die seriously and initially I would try to talk the person down, express love and concern for them and help them get through the next few hours, then hopefully their level of intoxification will decline, as will their level of suicidal thought, and call for help if possible. If the person has the means to commit suicide and is taking steps to do that, call the emergency services.'

Another highly distressing situation you can find yourself in is becoming the subject of physical violence. Alcohol can affect people in many different ways. In some cases they become incredibly docile and incapable of harming a flea, whilst in others they become terrifyingly aggressive. If your drinker is of the latter variety you should not rule out the possibility of another episode of violence rearing its head further down the line.

'The likelihood that your drinker will become violent is strongly related to her past behaviour. If she has been violent in the past, there is an excellent chance that violence will be part of the future.'

Robert J. Meyers and Brenda L. Wolfe from
Get Your Loved One Sober

In the event of being physically threatened you should have no hesitation in leaving the premises and, if you feel it appropriate, calling the police. There is a lot to be said for arranging a contingency plan with a friend or relative living locally who has a spare room.

Enabling Versus Tough Love

Another highly stressful area can be deciding on the appropriate level of support you should be offering and, as discussed in Chapter 1, there can be huge advantages to involving an objective third party to act as a sounding board because there is no universally correct answer. Much will depend on what stage the drinker's drinking career has reached, the underlying mental health issues involved and other particular circumstances of the case in question.

The majority of alcohol experts are quick to point to the dangers of 'enabling' the drinker, pointing out that although it will be your natural instinct to give in to their demands and tell them what they want to hear, this will actually hinder their chances of recovery and be detrimental to your own health. Drinkers must be encouraged to realize that they are responsible for their own destiny and to take responsibility for their own actions, and this involves loved ones setting clear boundaries.

'Boundaries are vital to recovery. Having and setting healthy limits is connected to all phases of recovery: growing in self-esteem, dealing with feelings and learning to really love and value ourselves. Boundaries emerge from deep within. They are connected to letting go of guilt and shame, and to changing our beliefs about what we deserve. As our thinking about this becomes clearer, so will our boundaries.'

Melody Beattie from *The Language of Letting Go*

Opinion is much more divided when it comes to the use of tough love and the idea of allowing the drinker to stew in their own juice until they reach 'rock bottom'. Some experts are adamant that recovery for any drinker is only possible if rock bottom is reached. Others stress that some people – but not others – will never start to recover until they have a near death experience, caused either by the alcohol itself or from an accident relating to it, such as a car accident or falling down the stairs. A third school of thought feels that early intervention with effective treatment is preferable to allowing a drinker to get anywhere near rock bottom.

Keith Burns of ADMIT Services is not a great believer in the concept of 'tough love': 'Parents, particularly mothers, find it extremely hard to throw their child on to the streets to fend for themselves, and problem drinkers can die long before "tough love" works. I really hate the term "rock bottom" because people's perception of where "rock bottom" is varies hugely. I was once contacted by the mother of a young girl selling sex for a pound out of the back of a car in a Bristol car park and their psychiatrist advised her mother to wait until her daughter reached rock bottom!'

As well as possibly resulting in tragedy for the drinker, waiting to reach rock bottom can virtually destroy the drinker's family, especially if they have not been paying sufficient attention to looking after themselves. Then again, if you are continually bailing them out financially or driving hundreds of miles to the rescue every time they need to be taken in for a detox you could be guilty of the very worst kind of enabling. So the decision as to whether or not you should refuse support is one that should not be taken lightly and the more opinions you can consult at the time, from suitably qualified professionals and from those with similar experiences, the better.

Jeffrey Huttman PhD from Challenges says, 'The answer depends on the circumstances surrounding the individual and is one of the most difficult decisions a family member can face. The results of giving up and severing support for a loved one continuing to drink could be the necessary step to stop the enabling process and force wellness. On the other hand, those with significant co-occurring mental health difficulties could potentially engage in increased self-destructive and harmful behaviour without family support, and the results could end tragically.'

Huttman stresses that, as a treatment professional, he could never make this decision for a family member, due to the risks involved. He therefore suggests that loved ones seek their own support in the form of therapy and/or Al-Anon, where they will get clarification in their decision making process through weighing up the circumstances as well as assistance from people who have been similarly affected.

It is generally acknowledged amongst experts that it's easier for a partner or spouse to break off contact with a drinker than it is for a blood relative to do so, although we have certainly come across cases where family members threatening disownership has resulted in drinkers quitting alcohol when everything else had failed. Those who distance themselves from blood relatives with drink problems also frequently find that it benefits themselves even if it doesn't reduce the drinker's alcohol intake.

■ **CASE STUDY** Son Realizes Tough Love is the Only Way for Him

Thirty-three-year-old Paul Jelf admits that he didn't notice anything untoward about his father's drinking until after his parents split up when he was aged eleven. However, when he visited the cottage his father moved into following the divorce he often found that his father slurred his words and bumped into things. On one occasion, when Paul was fourteen, his father even asked him who he was when he was helping him into bed.

Paul, who lives in Edinburgh, never mentioned the situation to anyone except his older sister Kate, who is now thirty-five. She often accompanied him on his visits to the cottage and on one occasion they went through his father's coat pockets together and found them stuffed full of half-bottles of vodka. It was even considered inappropriate to discuss the matter with their mother, whom they both lived with at the time, even though she was clearly aware of the problem.

By the age of fifteen the secrecy was beginning to have

an adverse affect on Paul by forcing him to bottle up his emotions, and things only got worse when he went to live with his father a year later. A couple of spells in rehab ensured that there were at least some sober periods, but these never lasted for more than a few months and, apart from the weeks when his father was actually in or had just left rehab, his drinking remained a largely taboo subject.

'If you tried to mention it he quickly got off the subject and he would always attribute his behaviour to the Valium he'd been prescribed by his GP to cope with the trauma of the divorce. Every time I went back home I was afraid that I would find him drinking and, when he met his second wife about eighteen months after I moved in, I was kind of delighted that there was someone else to deal with it.

'He certainly wasn't very honest with her and never admitted to her that he had a drink problem. Although I could see she noticed it, she never mentioned it. He always referred to her as his "higher power" and claimed that because of her he had his drinking under control. But his idea of having things under control was having four to six large cans of super-strength lager and about a quarter of a bottle of whisky every single day!'

'He had at some point chosen to open a bottle and decided that doing that was more important than his relationship with me.'

Unfortunately, Paul's stepmother died of cancer five years ago and his father went 'spectacularly off the rails' after her death, spending further time in rehab, getting asked to retire early from work and staging a suicide attempt. Since then there has been a fundamental breakdown in the relationship between father and son as a result of Paul realizing that he needed to pay more attention to his own wellbeing and happiness.

Splitting up with his long-term girlfriend four years ago was the catalyst because the situation was a result of Paul's emotional coldness, which in turn was caused by his father's drinking. Moving to a new home two and a half hours away from his where his father lived shortly afterwards made it easier for him to put his desire to be more detached into practice. Although Paul had moved out of his father's home eighteen months after his second marriage, he had only ever been a twenty-minute drive away.

'I had been made aware through friends that my cold behaviour wasn't normal,' explains Paul, 'but it had become a question of whether my life was more important than his. He had at some point chosen to open a bottle and decided that doing that was more important than his relationship with me. It was a difficult decision, but not one that I regret, and I am often telling people in similar situations to walk away and take away the safety net.'

'Frankly, it had become a question of whether my life was more important than his.'

'I wouldn't say that I've completely solved my problem of not being intimate in relationships, but I'm in a much healthier place right now and I have a new girlfriend who doesn't find me cold. I have become much more accepting of his situation now that I've realized that my life is not interlinked with his. He couldn't seem to get out of trouble without me and my sister helping out, and I was always taking him to hospital. So it's been important to break that cycle of him taking over my life.

'Kate is still providing a safety net and hindering his

recovery,' he continues, 'but I think she is beginning to get wiser now that she has three kids. At his rehab clinic we both went to the same family therapy sessions and they told us to let him get to rock bottom, but I think she has found it harder than me and you wonder at what point his rock bottom will come. The suicide attempt was clearly just a cry for help as the medics revealed that the amount of Paracetamol he took wasn't enough to kill someone. I would like to have a relationship with him, but I don't think it will happen as there is a fundamental lack of trust.'

Leaving a Partner

Experts commonly observe that family members rarely totally withdraw and, because they experience a lot of guilt, are likely to go on trying to rescue their child or relative, even if they know it isn't sensible. This certainly tallies with the feedback we've had from the parents of drinkers. One middle-aged lady with a twenty-year-old son told us, 'I could never turn the tap off completely, even though I want to kill him at times. When he's sober he is so charming and intelligent and attracts people towards him, and I will never forget that I brought a child into the world and I can't forget his sense of loneliness and isolation.'

Separation or divorce is, however, generally acknowledged to be a logical step to consider if all else fails, though a lot may depend on how long you've been with the person and the extent, if at all, to which they were adversely affected by alcohol when you first met them. If you have seen the 'whole person' originally, or a least a significant part of them, untainted by booze, you are far more likely to want the whole person back.

Professor Griffith Edwards of the National Addiction Centre, King's College London, says, 'Whether someone wants to stay in their marriage or get out is one of the big questions, and I feel that it is very reasonable for someone who is suffering from living with a problem drinker to contemplate breaking the marriage. But they may want to give the matter time and possibly wait for a few months to see if anything improves.'

As we have explained in Chapter 1, there is a difference between disowning someone completely, and detaching and ceasing to be responsible for them, but leaving the lines of communication open should they choose to help themselves. We strongly recommend the latter course of action, although at the end of the day the choice is obviously entirely yours. It may well be that you are in a new relationship and, if your current partner wants you to sever all connections, you may feel it's appropriate to do so. If you do this, however, at least make it clear to your former partner that it's their drinking you dislike as opposed to them as a person.

If someone is feeling very low, it's impossible to overestimate the importance of knowing that they at least have someone they can write to, email or phone up occasionally if they decide they are finally going to make a go of things. You don't have to listen for long and you can set firm boundaries about when and how often you can be contacted, but just leaving the door very slightly open, rather than slamming it shut, can be the difference between keeping the life-support machine on and switching it off.

For example, one middle-aged lady we met had left her partner of twenty-one years only weeks previously after finally deciding enough was enough. She had decided not to help him any more and that she wouldn't do so 'even if he complained he was excreting blood'. Nevertheless, she admitted that she still sometimes listened on the occasions when he phoned up drunk at two o'clock in the morning. At the end of the day that small concession could make the difference between life and death.

In some cases, when partners and spouses leave drinkers it turns out to be the trigger the drinker needs to finally go dry. This in turn can lead to a reconciliation between the couple (see the case study of Rahul and Rajeshwari Luther on pages 119 to 123), though it is by no means the norm.

We asked drinkers who have finally quit because, for example, their doctor said they would die if they didn't, whether it would have made them go dry earlier if their partner had threatened to leave them. None said it would have done, some said it definitely wouldn't have done, as they used to put drink before everything, and some said it wasn't a question they felt able to answer. This can be contrasted with our next question – what effect would it have had being advised in a direct manner by a friend or loved one that they had a drink problem? All those questioned agreed that it wouldn't have made them stop, rather they would simply have made more effort to hide their alcohol consumption.

■ **CASE STUDY** Support After Separation

Like most young women on her wedding day, Julie Hobson expected to remain married until the day she died. Furthermore, it never even entered her head that the man she was marrying might develop a serious drink problem.

Unfortunately, in November 2009, Julie finally decided to separate from her fifty-six-year-old husband, Ian, who had totally worn her out with his drinking and for whom she had lost all respect. Fortunately, the move and her subsequent behaviour seem to have at least contributed to his new-found sobriety.

> 'I care about him, and even if I began a new relationship I would, on principle, still want to show him support, assuming my new partner was OK about it.'

Julie, a fifty-seven-year-old receptionist, had been married to Ian for thirty-two years and admits that she didn't notice anything particularly untoward about his drinking to start with. When she first met him he had merely seemed a hearty social drinker who was proud of his ability to hold his drink and to drink anyone under the table. He was quite proud of the fact that he would always be the last person to leave the bar, even though Julie would sometimes point out that this wasn't necessarily something to be terribly proud of.

As Ian's job as a freelance engineer began to prove increasingly stressful in his early forties, drink gradually started to take over and eventually he couldn't do without a drink of whisky from a hip flask on the way to work, saying that otherwise he would have panic attacks on the train. By the age of fifty-two drink had impacted so adversely on his work that his contracts had dried up and they were entirely reliant on Julie's modest income in order to pay the bills.

Julie, who has three grown-up children, says, 'I tried saying that I didn't want anything to do with him and moving into the other bedroom, but it didn't work and, although I did manage to persuade him to go to AA for very short periods, he soon decided it wasn't for him and relapsed.

Every time he drank he ended up back in hospital and, unable to keep his food down, he frequently threw up blood. As soon as they detoxed him he would come out of hospital, but he didn't really get any support psychologically from anyone except from myself.

'Because he hadn't worked for five years we had to sell our home to manage financially,' she explains, 'and I gave him an ultimatum that if he didn't shape up before we found a buyer then we were going our separate ways. The house took twenty months to sell and during that time he'd chalked up twelve hospital stays and detoxes. In retrospect I feel I left it far too long as he was constantly falling over when drunk. On one occasion he broke his ankle, whilst on another he split his head open.'

In February 2010, only three months after they split, Ian spent four weeks in residential rehab. Although he was drinking again within a week of coming out, the coping skills he'd learned in rehab appear to be helping him as he has been dry for the last two months. The turning point seemed to come after Julie demonstrated a further piece of tough love.

> 'I remembered what I had been advised to say by the rehab people and told him that because he'd managed to phone me he could also manage to phone an ambulance.'

'He phoned me late one night saying he needed help and asking if I could get him to hospital, but I remembered what I had been advised to say by the rehab people, so I told him that because he'd managed to phone me he could also manage to phone an ambulance. By the time he got to hospital he was in a very bad way and I think he thought he was going to die. He still wears the plastic name tag they put on him in hospital and he says this is his reminder not to drink any more.

'It's so difficult when you've got someone you love asking you for help and you have to turn around and invite them to do it themselves, but on that occasion it seemed to work. He's lost all his friends and now sees only me and, very occasionally now that he's sober, the children.

'I would never go back to him but I care about him, and even if I began a new relationship I would, on principle, still want to show him support, assuming my new partner was OK about it.'

More Formalized Approaches

Informal attempts at trying to coax a drinker into seeking help tend to start off by avoiding confrontation and trying to strike a balance between offering simple caring support and avoiding enabling. Threats to disown or leave or other forms of confrontation tend to come later when the more subtle approaches have failed. We would suggest that it makes sense to try the more formalized methods for dealing with a drinker which focus on avoiding confrontation before considering family intervention, which centres on confrontation.

FRAMES

FRAMES is an approach commonly used in the alcohol addiction field to convince someone of the importance of overcoming that all-important first hurdle and accepting the fact that they might have a drink problem. Its title is an acronym for the techniques that need to be implemented: **F**eedback, **R**esponsibility, **A**dvice, **M**enu of Options, **E**mpathy and **S**elf-Efficacy.

These core techniques of motivational interviewing (MI) or motivational enhancement therapy (MET) are more difficult for the friends and loved ones of a drinker to use than they are for a professional, because those close to the drinker are likely to be emotionally involved with them to some extent. You must therefore do your best to stand back from any unpleasant feelings of anger or irritation that the drinker's behaviour triggers in you.

Dryoutnow.com's Dr Bruce Trathen says, 'Someone is much more likely to do something if they feel it has been their own decision rather than an order from someone else, or that they have to do it just to keep someone else happy. The essential trick is therefore to get the person to believe that they have made their own decision to seek help, and hopefully they really will make their own decision. Your role will be to help them reach a stage in their thinking process at which they are able to make that decision.'

He stresses that you won't achieve this by lecturing, bullying or begging, but by developing a certain attitude in your interactions with the person. By implementing the FRAMES techniques you will learn this attitude over time. It won't come naturally at first, but if you keep on trying it will eventually become second nature.

FEEDBACK

In feeding back information to the drinker your aim should be to highlight inconsistencies in the statements they make in a way that does not engender a feeling of resistance. If you find yourself disagreeing with what the drinker says or noticing that the problems they're blaming on other things are in fact due to their own behaviour, then it's important to neither directly disagree with them nor pretend to agree with them. Try to avoid making statements of fact and, if possible, ask open-ended questions – although closed questions requiring a 'yes' or 'no' answer are even better than statements of fact. Try to 'roll along' with the drinker, and avoid becoming resistant or defensive in response to what they say and giving in to them.

Through a mixture of open-ended and closed questions and a reasonably emphatic response, you may lead the drinker to conclude that they are not happy with themselves and that drinking might be the cause of their problem. Highlighting ambivalence in their statements and feelings will hopefully leave them with this nagging doubt.

For example, 'So let me check that I understand what you are saying. You are extremely keen on personal fitness but you habitually smoke and drink? Have I got that right?' If they say 'no', then ask them to correct you. If, on the other hand, they say 'yes', then leave it at that because you have increased their internal ambivalence and their discomfort with their own reasoning.

RESPONSIBILITY

You mustn't allow the drinker's determination and need to convince you that they don't have a problem to make you believe it's your problem. If someone is to make real progress they should take responsibility for the problems in their life, whether they relate to their drinking or not. Don't blame them for having problems; try to encourage them to take responsibility for their actions.

Avoid either hindering or helping and allow the natural conse-quences of the drinker's behaviour to occur. This way you should maximize the chances of the drinker actively experiencing prob-lems resulting from their drinking and in turn realizing that they have no one to blame but themselves. For example, if they are physically sick, invite them to clear up their own vomit, and decline requests to buy drink for them, but leave any drink they have bought for themselves where it is. This will be especially hard to achieve if you are living with the drinker or are emotionally involved with them. Nonetheless, it represents the way forward.

EMPATHY

Try to understand the drinker's feelings, but at the same time avoid sympathizing with them or criticizing them. If you can share an empathetic understanding of some kind they are far more likely to drop their guard and admit they might have a problem. Try to reconnect with any empathetic understanding you have shared in the past.

SELF-EFFICACY

Praising or rewarding the drinker for positive behaviour can enhance their own sense of their ability to change things for the better. This in turn will help them take responsibility for sorting out their own problems. So, just as you should ignore undesired behaviour, you should reward positive behaviour. You have to be subtle in your approach, though, otherwise the drinker might see through it and find it patronizing.

ADVICE AND MENU OPTIONS

Giving advice on ways in which the person can move forwards is the final stage, but it's vital you don't start giving advice until the person indicates they are receptive. Giving advice too early could push the drinker further into denial.

Once this stage has been reached, you could give them options that will enable them to receive an independent view on whether they do in fact have a drink problem. You could, for example, leave suitable information for the drinker to browse, and mention the possibility of them visiting their GP or making an appointment to see a counsellor. Make sure you give a range of options, though, because it's up to the drinker to make the decision, and if you leave only one option the decision has effectively become yours as opposed to the drinker's.

If the drinker chooses not to pursue any of the options, don't force the issue but, because the drinker has been prepared to acknowledge they might have a problem, it will be easier to bring the issue up again in the future.

EXERCISING PATIENCE

When using FRAMES try hard not to take on the role of the professional helper yourself and make sure that you don't rush anything. It is important to bide your time and wait for the appropriate responses. More detailed information on how to use FRAMES, including role plays, can be found at www.dryoutnow. com or by calling dryoutnow.com on 0845 460 1111.

CRAFT

CRAFT is an acronym for the Community Reinforcement and Family Training therapeutic model, which uses behavioural principles to reduce a drinker's alcohol misuse and to encourage them to seek treatment. It also aims to help the loved ones reduce stress and introduce meaningful sources of satisfaction into their lives. Unlike many other approaches, it does not teach detachment, but tries instead to make that relationship work.

A procedure known as 'behavioural mapping' underlies almost every strategy, providing a way of working out how drinkers and loved ones affect each other and how this pattern can be modified to achieve different results. Mapping interactions enables you to understand what has been triggering difficulties, then other techniques help you learn ways to stop your enabling behaviour, modify the drinker's behaviour and improve your communication and problem-solving capabilities.

'Open yourself up to new ways of interacting with your loved one and have the courage to take control of your situation. Rather than continually knocking your head against the same old walls, come along with us and learn how to control your reactions to your loved one and, through your reactions, shape a change in her behaviour.'

Robert J. Meyers and Brenda L. Wolfe from
Get Your Loved One Sober

The methods are based on the fact that family members and other people important to the drinker are the most influential people in the drinker's life. If you have lived with someone for years you are likely to have unusually strong insights into their habits. Indeed, you could even know them better than they know themselves. The fact that you may have a unique knowledge of their drinking patterns makes you exceptionally well placed to nudge their behaviour in directions you want it to go.

The road map describes the drinking triggers and early signs of intoxication. It also shows the consequences of a loved one's drinking, including any positive ones. Once you have all this information to hand you can begin to make changes, but it is also considered essential that you improve your own quality of life by introducing some good times into each day. Such self-reward can range from simply saying nice things to yourself to time away from chores with a good novel or even a professional massage.

Further Information on CRAFT can be obtained from *Get Your Loved One Sober: Alternatives to Nagging, Pleading, and Threatening* by Robert J. Meyers and Brenda L. Wolfe (Hazelden 2004).

Behavioural Couples Therapy

Another method involving behavioural principles, aimed specifically at spouses and partners who have been co-habiting for at
least a year, is Behavioural Couples Therapy. This uses a series of
behavioural assignments to increase relationship factors considered conducive to sobriety, such as positive feelings, shared
activities and constructive communication. This cannot simply be
carried out by loved ones on their own, though, as it requires the
involvement of a therapist. The drinker is asked for permission to
contact the spouse and the therapist then talks directly to the
spouse and invites them to sessions.

The behavioural approach assumes that those in more cohes-
ive relationships with better communication have a lower risk of
relapse. Typically, the drinker and spouse are seen together for
twelve to twenty outpatient sessions over three to six months and
the approach can be done either in isolation or in conjunction
with other counselling.

The drinker and partner arrange a daily sobriety contract in
which the drinker states their intention not to drink and the
partner expresses support for the drinker's efforts to remain
abstinent. If the drinker is taking any medication to help
combat their drink problem, taking this is also reinforced in
the contract. So, usually, is attendance at self-help group
meetings.

Initial sessions normally involve assessing the extent of the
alcohol abuse, the state of the relationship and gaining commitment to start the therapy. To begin with the focus is largely on the
drinking itself but, once abstinence and attendance have been
stable for a month or so, a start is made on relationship-focused
interventions in order to increase positive activities and teach
communication.

'"There's a good trick that people in dysfunctional relationships use," said one recovering woman. "The other person
does something inappropriate or wrong, then stands there

until you feel guilty and end up apologizing." It's imperative that we stop feeling so guilty.'

Melody Beattie from *The Language of Letting Go*

The partner records how the daily contract has been complied with on a calendar provided and both parties agree not to discuss either past drinking or fears about future drinking when at home in order to prevent conflicts that could trigger a relapse. Such discussions are saved for the actual therapy sessions. At the start of each session the sobriety contract is reviewed to see how well each partner has complied and progress is rewarded verbally at each session.

Sessions include reviewing urges to drink during the past week, including thoughts and temptations that are milder than actual urges and cravings. Discussion of situations, thoughts and feelings associated with urges helps to identify potential triggers or cues for alcohol abuse and can help flag up possible risks of relapse. It can also identify potential coping strategies for resisting urges and increasing future confidence.

Because relationships involving problem drinking can often become tense and unhappy, sessions aim to increase positive feeling, goodwill and commitment to the relationship and to teach communication skills to resolve conflicts, problems and desires for change.

For example, a 'Catch your partner doing something nice' approach asks partners to notify and acknowledge one pleasing behaviour performed by the drinker every day, and 'caring day assignments' require each partner to plan ahead to surprise the other with a day when they do something special to show they care. Planning and sharing rewarding activities involve both partners and their children or other adults, because many drinkers' families have stopped shared activities that are associated with positive recovery outcomes.

Family Intervention

Family Intervention provides a way of 'raising the bottom' before rock bottom occurs via a well-planned process in which family members join in lovingly but firmly to confront the drinker about their drink problem and impress upon them the necessity of them seeking treatment. The drinker's close friends and employer are also often involved.

Experts tend to talk in terms of 80 per cent to 90 per cent success rates, if success is defined as motivating the drinker to accept help, but the approach obviously involves significant risks, so it's important that it's planned in conjunction with appropriate professional advice, although the doctor, or 'interventionist', doesn't necessarily have to be present at the session itself.

Although members of the family may have known that the drinker had a problem for years this is likely to be the first time the family has come together as a group and talked about the problem and its solution. Most people never experience a time when the people they care about come together in one room at one time to tell them how much they love them and why, so it can be a highly traumatic and emotional encounter for someone who is used to feeling distinctly unlovable.

'Through our work on intervention, we have found that love is a powerful force when confronting addiction. In the past, expressions of love were delegated to a few brief sentences during an intervention. We've learned that when we expand the role of love, it is love, rather than toughness, that first breaks through denial.'

Jeff Jay and Debra Jay from *Love First*

Another reason for the success of this approach is that the drinker finally hears how their addiction has affected the people who love them. Because emotions can run high on such occasions it is normal for members of the team to read from pre-written statements rather than try to come up with appropriate words on the day.

Even if the drinker refuses help, the fact that they have received these words offered by family and friends should linger in their consciousness for a long time. The idea is that because they can't forget them it should profoundly affect their future drinking. The drinker also learns that those closest to them no longer intend to enable the disease, but that each one has instead made a commitment to support only recovery. They are told that they can turn to anyone in the group at any time and that they will do anything they can to help with their recovery.

Considerable preparation is required, with an essential starting point being the compilation of a list of all the people the drinker loves, needs, admires, respects, likes and relies on. The team will normally consist of between three and nine members, but it is important to exclude anyone the drinker intensely dislikes, anyone with a drink or other addiction-related problem and anyone likely to spill the beans by tipping off the drinker in advance about what is supposed to be a surprise event. The event should take place somewhere other than in the drinker's home, unless its clearly impossible to get the drinker to go anywhere.

It is important to involve a doctor experienced in alcohol issues but, unless they are a close family friend, they are likely to provide a written recommendation for a member of the team to read out as opposed to attending themselves. Although doctors often fail to make much progress during one-to-one sessions with drinkers, their recommendations are capable of being more powerful when read out during an intervention.

Anyone entering into this approach should do so with their eyes open, as there could be tragic consequences if things backfire. In particular, be aware of the importance of arranging an intervention to coincide with when the family, especially the drinker's partner, are ready for it.

'The problem arises when a spouse is not yet ready to go through an intervention. To try and make a spouse opt for an intervention too early in her recovery is not a good idea. Let me say here that *most* interventions are successful: *when* the family is *ready* for them. Far better, in such circumstances, for the spouse of the alcoholic to be encouraged to wait until she is ready to face the consequences of an intervention.'

Toby Rice Drews from *Getting Them Sober, Volume 2*

Involving a professional interventionist is especially important if the drinker has problems that extend beyond their drinking, has a history of mental illness, violence or attempting or threatening suicide, or has had a number of previous treatments but relapsed. It may also be appropriate if relationships with family and friends have deteriorated so badly that there is no one to fill the chairman's role.

Furthermore, although Family Intervention may be worth considering in the UK in certain circumstances, it is unlikely to appeal to those who don't like a direct talking approach. It is therefore probably culturally more appropriate in the US.

Further information can be obtained from the website, www.associationofinterventionspecialists.org and from *Love First* by Jeff Jay and Debra Jay (Hazelden Foundation, 2008).

After the Turning Point – Going Forward

Even if you have managed to help the individual come to the realization that they need help and they have gone dry as a result of benefiting from one or more of the treatment methods outlined in Chapters 5 and 6, for the first couple of years you can only consider yourself to have won the battle rather than the war. You are therefore likely to have a hugely important part to play in the former drinker's ongoing recovery for some considerable time.

'Understanding that the alcoholic's brain takes from one to three years to return to "normal" is hugely important to your wellbeing. It will explain some of the alcoholic's behaviours and help you to adjust your expectations that "all will be well" once they've stopped drinking. It will also help you to tolerate a slip without giving up in despair.'

Lisa Frederiksen from *If You Loved Me You'd Stop!*

Furthermore, it's important to realize that the relationship you enjoy with the former drinker going forward is likely to be significantly different from the one you experienced before, especially if the individual concerned is a spouse or live-in partner. In addition to taking steps to help your own happiness and wellbeing, you might find you have to make compromises for the sake of maintaining a healthy relationship.

We have noticed, in particular, that those who have recently overcome drink problems and are managing to remain dry frequently complain that they used to be the life and soul of the party and are concerned that people now find them rather dull. Unfortunately, although we have seen that those who drink to excess can turn people right off without realizing it (see Chapter 3), there is also a fair amount of truth in their complaint. Alcohol does break down inhibitions and can make people more jovial and even hysterically funny at times.

One forty-year-old man told us, 'When I was drinking I could get very angry at the slightest thing and so my relationship with my girlfriend was very volatile. Now it has levelled off and I haven't argued since I started the detox three weeks ago, but it has also detrimentally affected my relationship. I'm like a new man and not as passionate about things, and my girlfriend now feels a bit left out and feels the relationship is over as she's done her bit as a carer.'

A man of a similar age who had been dry for three months volunteered, 'Trust issues are still there and are always going to be, but I'm beginning to understand that it must be hard to believe someone who used to drink twelve cans of beer or a bottle of vodka a day. We are getting on much better, but my wife did say she was finding it more difficult to talk to me as I am now generally much more reflective and quiet.'

Even if the former drinker has no reservations about their new life, their partner can still be conscious of sacrifices they are having to make to accommodate them. A man in his early fifties told us, 'I was the life and soul and you are definitely a different person not drinking. But my relationship with my wife is much better because I don't talk a load of nonsense.'

It's not always plain sailing, however, and sometimes sacrifices will need to be made. His wife, who is of a similar age, said, 'When he was drinking he was in bed by seven or eight o'clock and I had all my TV programmes to watch; now I have to involve him in watching these. The rows we had when he was drinking were about really stupid pointless things such as should the toilet paper come from under or over the holder.'

It's also important to realize that, even if the former drinker doesn't actually suffer a relapse, their recovery period is likely to have peaks and troughs, and the troughs are likely to prove especially challenging for those closest to them.

'What's confusing sometimes is that the alcoholic will go along for a few weeks feeling good when all of a sudden the stress of withdrawal will hit again. What happens is that his withdrawal from the drug (of alcohol) goes through cycles of varying intensity. He can feel bad for a few months during early sobriety, then feel good, then feel bad again, and so on.'

Toby Rice Drews from *Getting Them Sober, Volume 2*

Dealing With Cravings

The most critical points of all are likely to be when the former drinker complains they are experiencing intense cravings for alcohol. As these can sometimes be associated with particular triggers, paying attention to when the drinker appears most susceptible to them can help indicate when you should be on red alert in the future. Cravings could, for example, be triggered by a stressful time at work, or even by something as seemingly minor as walking past a chocolate shop. A drinker is also likely to be more prone to them if they are in a vulnerable state as a result of something like a relationship breakdown.

As discussed in Chapter 2 (see page 28) one very significant way in which you should be able to help a drinker in their struggle to combat cravings is to point out that they are likely to reduce over time, so that if they can manage to resist them initially their life should eventually become much easier.

In our experience, those with drink problems are very often unaware of the fact that things can get easier with time in this respect and the idea that these cravings are a life sentence can make them take a very defeatist attitude that can result in relapse. Simply explaining that the longer they can hold out, the easier it is likely to become can make a massive contribution towards ensuring that they make a sustained recovery.

Many people with drink problems are also unaware that doctors and psychiatrists are able to prescribe medication that can help reduce cravings. As we see in Chapter 5, there is currently no one wonder drug commonly prescribed by conventional alcohol experts that can be guaranteed to remove cravings altogether, but there are a number of options that may make life easier for the sufferer. Letting the drinker know about this can help, as can telling them about counselling services, which suggest specific strategies for coping with cravings.

Professor John Saunders of Sydney University says, 'Those close to the problem drinker should be aware that complaining about cravings may be a way of them saying that he or she is not committed to dealing with their problem and is looking to legitimize their resumption of drinking. First I would ask the problem drinker to consider what life was like when drinking and how it has been since ceasing. I would also suggest they take appropriate medication to reduce their cravings, as well as learning or continuing to practise techniques to suppress the urges.'

Simply encouraging those trying to resist cravings to do something to divert their attention can also be of great benefit. This could range from doing crosswords and listening to favourite tracks on their CD player to having a non-alcoholic drink.

Peter Smith at Broadway Lodge says, 'Cravings can trip people up and can be triggered by any number of things and, unless you interrupt that process, you start a rolling snowball. Encourage them to do things that distract them and bear in mind that some things may work for some people but not for others. More people get cravings than don't, and somewhere in their mind something triggers off the thought of having a drink and this becomes what feels like a physical urge. Having a soft drink can show them it's not actually a physical thing.'

Encouraging those who suffer from cravings to attend AA (See Chapter 5, pages 126 to 130) can also prove extremely valuable. One of the reasons AA has proved successful for so many people with drink problems over the years is that when a member experiences cravings they can phone another member, who urges them not to drink, possibly reminding them that their own failure to resist cravings cost them their home and their livelihood and asking them whether they really want to end up in the same boat.

Jeffrey Huttman PhD from Challenges says, 'Family members wishing to be supportive of a loved one's abstinence are often faced with a difficult task because they are not usually in the best position to provide objective advice or recommendations, due to their close relationship with the individual who is struggling. However, simply conveying their support and reminding them of potential resources available to the recovering individual may be helpful. These include supporting the individual's attendance in 12-Step meetings such as AA, with sponsorship and a defined home group and support group.

'The individual experiencing cravings can be prompted to contact his or her sponsor or attend a meeting to get support with the cravings he or she is experiencing. Individual or group therapy, or treatment through a structured outpatient or inpatient programme may be necessary to treat continued abstinence and assist the individual in avoiding relapse.'

Some individuals we have spoken to who are managing to remain dry report that eating sweets or hamburgers or drinking Diet Coke really help when they are feeling an urge for a drink. Such tactics would certainly run contrary to the advice you'll get from a nutritionist, who is likely to point out that consuming sugar or artificial sweeteners is actually likely to increase cravings by making the brain feel it needs sugar or alcohol. Nevertheless, if a drinker finds a formula that works for them there's a lot to be said for allowing them to stick with it, at least initially.

We feel that telling people they are not allowed any treats for fear that they will become 'cross-addicted' to cream or chocolate can prove counter-productive in the same way as insisting they turn up to AA every single day for the first ninety days of recovery. At the end of the day each individual has got to find the formula that works best for them, even if it doesn't involve sticking rigidly to prescribed methodology.

Similarly, encouraging someone to do puzzles to take their mind off cravings can work wonders in some cases, but if that someone happens to hate puzzles it could greatly increase the chances of them wanting a drink. The emphasis should be on encouraging the pastime or habit that seems to be most effective at distracting that particular person.

One area in which we would urge caution, however, is in the use of alcohol substitutes. While we feel these can be a useful tool for those wishing to cut down or for pregnant women and others wishing to give up for brief periods, we feel there are definite risks for those wanting to remain dry as they can stimulate old drinking habits. So when someone who has kicked the drink complains that lemonade and steak don't go well together, we would advise thinking twice before volunteering they wash their next steak down with a bottle of de-alcoholized red.

Similarly, there is a lot to be said in the early stages for helping your drinker to avoid high-risk situations, such as weddings, funerals, pubs, rugby clubs and parties, and when they do go, you can provide important support by accompanying them.

> 'One of the best ways to combat the feeling of alienation we often experience at family or social events is to take along a sober friend. Having someone in the "trenches" with you is one of the most responsible actions you can do to safeguard your recovery and your state of mind.'
>
> Georgia W. from *Don't Let the Bastards Grind You Down*

Above all, put as much energy as possible into focusing on the positives of the drinker. Family members will know that the drinker is good at pulling out all the negatives, but there is a lot to be said for getting them all round the table one evening and making a list of the drinker's good points. For example, what qualifications have they got? What have they been good at? What have been their achievements, however small? What are their interests? Who have they ever come across who has inspired them? What are their most lovable personality traits? Such a session can collectively help family members and the drinker get down on paper what the drink has pushed out to the periphery. The list can then be added to by the drinker as and when.

▣ CASE STUDY A Miracle Made to Happen

Right from the start Rajeshwari Luther was somewhat aware of the effect that alcohol could have on the man she ended up marrying . . . twice. After all, she first met Rahul when he was being treated in a de-addiction centre she was working at in Bangalore, India, in 1987. Nevertheless, she convinced herself that he would eventually give up drinking for the sake of her love.

Two decades later her dream is very much alive and the couple are drawing on their past experiences to run Hope

Trust, one of India's top rehab clinics based in Hyderabad. But the road to sobriety for Rahul, now aged fifty-three, was a decidedly rocky one and his destination was only reached with the help of plenty of tough love.

'At first I just didn't understand how overwhelming his addiction had become,' admits Rajeshwari, who is now forty-four. 'He was a very talented copywriter, but ended up losing a number of jobs and started becoming embarrassing to be with when we went out. He would even come and embarrass me in front of my co-workers at my own workplace, and my overwhelming sensation was one of shame. But, like many addicts, he was also a charmer and could convince anyone about anything.'

'By constantly doing things for him I was decreasing his pain and increasing mine.'

Rahul had started drinking in the early 1970s when he was a student at Delhi University. Looking back, he puts it down to an attempt to fit in with the overwhelming wave of the hippie generation. He was impressed by the clothes and mannerisms, the music and thinking, in terms of free love, freedom and anti-establishment attitudes.

'I led a double life, drunk inside but functional outside,' he explains. 'My heroes were achievers like Richard Burton and Norman Mailer, who had led similar secret lives. The basic principle or belief was that I could get away with it. I was smarter, had a better way and would surely achieve my goals with my methods, which need not conform to established beliefs?

'Gradually my attitudes and behaviour started getting more intolerant, self-centred and grandiose. The frequency and quantity of alcohol increased and I guess things must have become ever more difficult for my newly wed wife. I became verbally abusive and constantly resentful of everyone, and I understand I even became physically violent on a couple of occasions, although I do not actually remember these incidents as a result of memory blackouts.'

Having settled in Delhi following their marriage in 1988, the couple became increasingly reliant on Rajeshwari's income from nursing and on financial assistance from Rahul's father, who was a high-ranking government employee. Rahul proved incapable of holding down a job for any length of time, despite receiving new opportunities through his father's contacts, although he chipped in with the odd bit of freelance copywriting work.

Rahul's drinking resulted in him socializing less and less and becoming increasingly stressed as he tried to pretend that everything was normal. His health was clearly deteriorating and in 1990 he brought things to a head when he became too drunk to be at his wife's bedside for the birth of his daughter Raisa.

'I can't even describe the hurt and humiliation that resulted from not having any support at Raisa's birth,' explains Rajeshwari, 'and the only thing I regret after all these years is the trauma Raisa had to go through as a child. Even though she has had counselling and occasionally attended Alateen meetings, at the age of twenty there is hardly any emotional bonding with her father. There is still a lot of approval seeking from him and she occasionally exhibits low self-esteem issues, despite having been sheltered and provided for.'

'Divorcing was an extremely hard decision as I still loved him at some level, but we simply couldn't have carried on like that and my daughter deserved better.'

As Rahul's behaviour increasingly took its toll, Rajeshwari indulged in a little emotional blackmail by taking frequent breaks at her parents' house. She kept threatening not to come back and not to allow him to see his daughter, but it was all to no avail, and on one occasion he even took their daughter away without permission for three days. Rajeshwari tried getting other family members to talk to him about his drink problem, but nothing seemed to work as he never had to face the consequences of his drinking.

'I don't think he believed I would be able to live without him,' she continues, 'especially as when I was away I used to still try and make sure he was OK by phoning the maid and checking that he was eating properly and that the house was clean. I was at the height of my co-dependency and, looking back, it was crazy as it wasn't doing any good. By constantly doing things for him I was decreasing his pain and increasing mine. But in those days I didn't know there was any help I could ask for.'

Eventually they moved to Hyderabad to stay with Rahul's parents, hoping things would improve, but the addiction actually grew worse. Indeed, it got so bad that Rahul's parents actually persuaded Rajeshwari to divorce him.

'Divorcing was an extremely hard decision as I still loved him at some level, but we simply couldn't have carried on like that and my daughter deserved better,' she explains. 'It was an act of sheer helplessness as I could not see any future with him and badly needed to consolidate a plan for my own survival. I was touched beyond measure when his parents offered to adopt me and to have me living with them as their own daughter, but I declined.'

However, she did hope that the move would change his thinking, and eventually she was proved correct. After Rahul's parents asked him to leave their home, he finally decided to undergo rehabilitation at a centre in Bangalore. As family counselling was an integral part of the treatment, Rajeshwari was invited to participate, too. Initially she refused as she was so full of anger, but when she eventually decided to cooperate she found that it helped her immensely and she learned how to de-victimize herself.

'Miracles don't just happen, you have to make them happen, and we succeeded.'

Meanwhile, Rahul made considerable progress with the therapy and started working in the facility. He proved that he wanted his family back badly enough to give up drinking, and Rajeshwari finally agreed to give him a second chance. In 2001 they re-married and had their second child, a boy they christened Rishabh.

His wife's ongoing support and his parents' tough love have been crucial factors in Rahul's continued sobriety. Rajeshwari ensured that Rahul continued to attend AA meetings and see a counsellor, often showing her appreciation of him by accompanying him and participating in his programmes. Between them they have learned to talk over his issues regularly.

'Even though we got remarried it still took me between eighteen months to two years to fully adjust to my husband being in recovery,' she recalls. 'I was still angry and he still had to adapt his behaviour. But the biggest single turning point was the birth of my son. This made Rahul settle down emotionally, financially and socially. He never bonded with his daughter, but having Rishabh helped him bond with people. Sobriety can be a struggle for a few years, especially with this lack of emotional expression.

'But I am very, very happy now. I couldn't have a better person in my life and I wouldn't trade him for anyone else. He goes to AA regularly and talks about AA all the time whilst he's working in rehab. Miracles don't just happen, you have to make them happen, and we succeeded.'

In summary

- Focus on your own happiness right from the outset

- When considering intervention approaches, the idea is to set a subtle example rather than appear judgemental, and methods that avoid confrontation should be tried before those using confrontation

- Meeting with some kind of resistance is inevitable when trying to proactively help, but you can reduce the level of resistance by approaching things in the right way

- Discuss your particular situation with as many relevant parties as possible and, if you decide to leave a drinker, try to leave the lines of communication open in case they decide to go dry

CHAPTER FIVE

Traditional Methods of Treatment and Help

A s we explained in Chapter 1, trying to find the right form of help for someone with a serious drink problem can be compared to having a bunch of keys without knowing which one fits their particular lock. You might have to keep trying one key after another until you come across the right one and, unfortunately, practitioners of approaches that have failed may be reluctant to provide guidance as to what you should try next.

Finding the right key can feel like a pretty lonely process. Even if you have taken our advice and tried to involve a third party, if that third party is a treatment professional wedded to any particular approach, there may come a time when you temporarily have to disregard their advice and consider some of the other options we mention. Whatever you do, don't conclude that there is no hope for your drinker just because the one or two approaches you have tried haven't worked.

'If the alcoholic returns to drinking, the family and friends should not give up, saying, "We tried treatment, and it didn't work." They should instead try to find a program that gives the alcoholic a better chance of recovery: and if that treatment fails, they should try again and again. While relapses are discouraging, they are not the end of the road. In fact, most alcoholics now sober have had at least one relapse on the way to lasting sobriety.'

James R. Milam and Katherine Ketcham from *Under the Influence*

Alcoholics Anonymous (AA)

By far the best known and most widely available source of external help available is AA, which is a fellowship of men and women who share experiences, strengths and hopes with each other to solve common problems and help others with drink problems. Wherever you are in the civilized world, the chances are that there is an AA group that meets within driving or even walking distance.

(For the UK see www.alcoholics-anonymous.org.uk, and for worldwide see www.aa.org). AA is fast growing in places as far removed from one another as Brazil and China, and it has even broken into the Muslim world through rapid growth in Iran.

AA was not founded by medics, but resulted from drinkers realizing they had a better chance of staying sober if they helped each other. It doesn't claim to provide a cure, but works on the principle that everyone with a drink problem suffers from a disease and that giving up drinking alcohol altogether represents the only solution.

Open meetings can be attended by those who have a desire to stop drinking, their families and anyone interested in helping those with drink problems, but the majority of the meetings available are closed ones, which are only for the drinkers themselves. In many cases a chairperson, after making an initial introduction, hands over to one or more other speakers, who talk about their battles with alcohol, and all who attend are subsequently free to make their own comments and observations about the problems they have experienced with alcohol and the successes they have enjoyed with remaining sober. Further informal discussions often take place at the end, over light refreshments such as tea or coffee and biscuits. No charge is made for attendance, although donations can be made by those who wish to.

Meetings allow detailed discussion of the recovery programme, the core principles of which are contained in the 12 Steps, which begin with the drinker admitting they are powerless over alcohol, that their lives have become unmanageable and that they believe a power greater than themselves can restore them to sanity.

Although the 12 Steps contain plenty of references to 'God', it is essential to recognize that AA is not a religious organization. It has a spiritual dimension, but that is not the same thing. It relates more to an ability to reach out for help and undergo a change in personality. All that is required is for drinkers to believe in a power greater than themselves, even if this is simply their AA group.

Those who manage to remain sober are able to do service, which may initially include helping with washing up and putting chairs away after meetings, making the tea/coffee and supplying the biscuits or acting as a greeter at meetings, especially looking for newcomers. They may in due course even be invited by the chairperson to give their story at a meeting.

As an organization that has already helped millions of people worldwide, it would be hard not to single out AA as being likely to represent the most appropriate starting point to consider for someone with a drink problem. It's anonymous, it's widely available, it's free and many people swear by it. Even if someone doesn't have a physical addiction and is only intending to give up alcohol for an initial period, attending AA can provide them with valuable social interaction and encouragement.

Doctors, therapists and rehab clinics commonly recommend that patients attend AA as an important part of their aftercare service. Indeed, most rehab clinics actually have treatment models based on their own slightly modified version of the 12 Steps.

It is in fact relatively commonplace for attendance at AA meetings to be one component of a broader treatment package, although long-time regular AA attenders, because they believe that only those with drink problems can help others with drink problems, are pretty cynical about the merits of rehab or of the medication that doctors or specialists may prescribe.

This can be off-putting and upsetting for someone who has just left rehab and is attending counselling, especially if they have been informed by doctors that they are suffering from an underlying medical condition such as depression or chronic anxiety. We feel that it is important that if you point someone in the direction of AA you make them aware of the possibility of experiencing such negativity.

You could advise that this is possibly one aspect of an otherwise largely excellent organization that has changed little in over seventy-five years and could therefore be viewed as a bit out of date. After all, it is now fairly common for staff at rehab clinics and therapists of all kinds in the alcohol addiction field to be former drinkers, and many of them swear by AA.

'A.A. is the best program in existence for helping alcoholics to stay sober, but it is not a particularly effective vehicle for getting the alcoholic sober in the first place. A.A. is not a treatment program because it has no detoxification facilities or staff, no twenty-four-hour medical care, no professional counselling services and no authority to ensure patient compliance with a treatment regime.'

James R. Milam and Katherine Ketcham from
Under the Influence

A further important message to get across is that simply attending the same AA meetings a few times or reading the 12 Steps does not qualify someone to make a fair assessment of the overall AA experience. Meetings can vary in terms of atmosphere and quality, so if someone is disenchanted with one meeting they've attended it's important that they try others.

To reap its maximum benefits those with drink problems should undergo the 12 Step programme in conjunction with a sponsor – an experienced AA attender who can use the benefit of their own experience to give valuable guidance. It should be possible to find a sponsor by asking around at local meetings or, failing this, ringing an AA helpline, but it is important not just to snatch at the first one available, as you need to have someone you can identify with. Feedback from people who go the whole hog and complete the 12 Step programme in conjunction with a suitable sponsor is invariably far more positive than feedback from dabblers.

Our own principal reservation about AA is that, whilst viewing someone with a physical addiction as having a disease can undoubtedly be extremely important, both in terms of helping them remain abstinent and helping those closest to them to detach, it can prevent those who have psychological addictions from moving on and putting their drink problems behind them.

Additionally, as we see in Chapter 6, there are now exciting new methods of treatment that aim to enable those with physical addictions to go back to drinking in moderation. The AA belief that there is no cure for alcoholism could therefore hinder an individual's progress. Our view in this respect is that if AA is clearly working then it's probably worth taking the view that 'if it ain't broke don't fix it'. If, on the other hand, someone has given AA a fair shot and is continually relapsing and questioning whether they should continue attending, then it may be worth trying something else.

The simple fact of the matter is that, whilst the 12-Step approach has radically transformed many people's lives for the better, it doesn't work for everyone. We know people who, although they have benefited to an extent from AA and from rehab, found that AA couldn't help them in the way that more modern methods could, and we have obviously come across further such individuals whilst writing up case studies for this book.

It is also important to realize that even if someone clearly doesn't benefit from the 12-Step-based approach it doesn't mean that they can't benefit from attending another form of self-help group.

Although not so widely available, SMART Recovery (www.smartrecovery.org) and SOS International (www.sossobriety.org)

provide non-12-Step-based alternatives to AA. There may also be local self-help groups in your drinker's area that are worth trying. These can be organized by local authorities, charities or even individual therapists. In some cases these may encourage drinkers to be accompanied by partners or family members, enabling you to make a contribution that goes well beyond mere recommendation.

▇ CASE STUDY Helping on a Number of Fronts

Considering he doesn't drink much himself, alcohol has played a surprisingly large part in the life of sixty-seven-year-old Steve Wilson, who has had to deal with drink problems affecting his mother, his business partner and his second wife. Although the experiences have clearly been traumatic, he is able to look back with some pride at the way his own actions have helped instigate several recoveries.

Whilst he didn't seem to be able to do much to turn his mother's life around, he made a huge contribution towards the eventual sobriety of the other two by referring them to AA, and by taking the decision to attend Al-Anon Steve also did much to improve his own wellbeing and happiness.

His father having disappeared from the scene when he was only five years old, Steve was brought up by a mother he adored and a very domineering grandmother against whose criticisms he was constantly defending his mother. Between the ages of eighteen and twenty-one, when he was living with them both while attending university, the subject of his mother's drinking began to rear its head as his grandmother constantly complained she was drinking too much.

'She had quite a big plastic tumbler which you couldn't see through because it had a pattern on it, and she used to drink whisky from this,' recalls Steve, who currently has a partner and three adult children. 'I always stuck up for my mother and, whilst I was living at home, her drinking never seemed to be the issue to me. I thought the real problems were my grandma and my mother's health. Mum always seemed to have lots of health problems, coupled with deep unhappiness, and in my twenties her drinking became heavier and she used alcohol as a sort of anaesthetic.'

Even when he finally realized that she had a serious drink problem neither he nor anyone else could persuade her to go to AA. Eventually, after his grandmother had to be put in a home, his mother sold her house and came to live next door to him in South London. By this time he had got married and had two children. She didn't go out much and just seemed intent on drinking herself to death. By the age of sixty-nine she succeeded, after developing cirrhosis of the liver.

'At Al-Anon I realized I had to address myself and my response to her drinking.'

Steve, who was forty-seven at the time of her death, recalls, 'To tell her that drink was killing her didn't seem to be a threat as she wasn't happy and clearly wanted to die. In her very final year we did go and see a drugs and alcohol counsellor together in Mayfair. The counsellor, who had specifically requested to see me as well, asked me if Mum's drinking bothered me and I said it did. Mum was furious and wouldn't allow me to accompany her again, but she continued to go herself and had actually just checked into a rehab clinic shortly before she died. Unfortunately, she didn't live long enough to get there.'

Only nine months after his mother's death Steve received a phone call pleading for help from the wife of Martin, his business partner in the film industry. Martin's long-standing drink problem had escalated out of control and he was ranting and raving like a lunatic. Despite Steve's experience with his own mother and realizing that his colleague drank too much and suffered from severe mood swings, he hadn't twigged that it was much of an issue. In particular, he'd had no idea that the large amounts of orange juice he'd always seen Martin consume were in fact laced with vodka.

Martin had been very close to Steve's mother, so Steve took him to visit her grave, hoping that it would do the trick. His hunch proved correct and Martin immediately volunteered that he wanted to quit alcohol altogether. Steve gave him the phone numbers of two former problem drinkers he knew who had been dry for many years as a result of attending AA. Martin phoned them and they told him to attend AA.

Steve went to an AA meeting with Martin the next day and, seeing the positive effect it had on his friend, he insisted that Martin live at his house for the next two weeks and accompanied him to a meeting every single day during that time. He would barely let him out of his sight during this period, effectively holding him prisoner. As a result Martin quit the drink and has remained dry for twenty years since.

'Steve gave him the phone numbers of two former problem drinkers he knew who had been dry for many years as a result of attending AA. Martin phoned them and they told him to attend AA.'

Having now failed to spot the signs of problem drinking in two people close to him, lightning was about to strike for a third time. Barely six months after accompanying his friend to AA, Steve left his wife of ten years in order to begin a passionate affair with Mary, an Irish lady he had met whilst away on business. The couple soon married and Mary and her six-year-old daughter from a previous relationship moved to London.

'At first I didn't think much about her heavy drinking because it didn't seem terribly out of place in Ireland,' continues Steve, 'but I began to notice how unreliable she was and that she didn't look after her daughter properly. Love makes you blind, though, and when I raised the subject of her drinking, she said it wasn't a problem.'

The marriage was rocky pretty much from the word go as Mary never made any serious attempt to find work and Steve soon found out she had a history of manic depression. He gave her the number for AA and invited her to phone it, saying that it was a key to a door that could change her life. She refused, despite being aware of how it had helped Martin, because she was very cynical about such programmes, but she did put the number in her wallet.

Almost exactly a year later Mary paid a secret visit to AA and, by a strange coincidence, it was on the very same day that Steve made a secret visit of his own to Al-Anon, a 12-Step-based self-help group for the loved ones of problem drinkers. From then on Mary attended AA every day and, with the exception of one slip-up, remained dry right up until she returned to Ireland five years later after the couple divorced, at which point communication ceased. Steve also continued to attend Al-Anon and found the experience invaluable.

'He gave her the number for AA and invited her to phone it, saying that it was a key to a door that could change her life.'

'At Al-Anon I realized I had to address myself and my response to her drinking,' he recalls. 'Even though Mary had gone dry, her behaviour hadn't changed. She had huge mood swings and was very antagonistic towards my children from my first marriage. I realized that I was the type of person who can't say no and was always needy. I also became aware that I had a huge ego, which was standing in the way of my serenity, and realized that undergoing the 12 Steps involved a gradual dismantling of this ego.

'I felt this extraordinary liberation from realizing that I didn't have to be responsible for other people. I'd always been responsible for my mother and my partners, and I finally recognized that the most important person to look after was myself, and that by doing so it enabled me to look after other people in a more healthy way. My wife turned really nasty on me during the divorce and during that period my son was sectioned and had a schizophrenic episode. It paid off that I could be helpful in the right way and give him the help and support he needed without trying to control him, and it made me realize I had always tried to control others rather than help them in a healthy way.'

Medication

A number of medications are currently available worldwide to deter those with drink problems from touching alcohol or to help them reduce their cravings. There is nothing to stop these being taken in conjunction with attendance at AA.

Jeffrey Huttman PhD at Challenges says, 'There have been some novel advances in the field of addiction medicine that can be extremely helpful to the recovering individual who needs more assistance to maintain abstinence and reduce cravings than attendance at 12-Step meetings and therapeutic treatment.

'However, medication should be carefully chosen with the prescription of a psychiatrist who specializes in addiction and not by GPs, who may be limited in their experience with them. Not everybody attempting sobriety requires medication to accomplish their goals and, as with many prescription medications, the potential rewards need to outweigh the potential side effects.'

Nevertheless, it is important not to present these more conventional forms of medication to the drinker as some form of magical cure. Unlike the more revolutionary and less researched newer methods discussed in Chapter 6, even those who prescribe these are lukewarm about the potential benefits.

Furthermore, there is no shortage of alcohol experts who hesitate to recommend any of these established forms of medication. Some have simply found they don't tend to do much good, whereas others feel that, even if they can provide modest benefits, they are not conducive to a longer-term recovery.

Peter Smith at Broadway Lodge says, 'We would be looking at getting everybody off everything. The likelihood is that if other chemicals are impacting on their life it increases the likelihood of them wanting alcohol in the long run and more medication in the long run.'

We are also keen to point out that if a form of medication is clearly proving beneficial there is much to be said for sticking with it at least in the short term. We feel that over-emphasizing the perils of cross-addiction can sometimes hamper immediate progress and that it is better for someone to be dependent on medication if it enables them to lead a reasonably normal life than it is to be homeless and unable to function as a result of problem drinking.

Arguably the most controversial of the established medications used for combating alcohol addiction is Antabuse (also known as disulfiram). Normally taken as a pill – although in some countries other than the UK it is available as an implant – this causes an unpleasant and sometimes even dangerous reaction if someone drinks alcohol while taking it. The obvious downside is that, armed with this knowledge, those wanting to drink alcohol can all too easily opt out of talking their pill.

'Everyone's experience is different, but for me, Antabuse was a short-term solution. If you are going to take it you *have* to be self-motivated, because if you drink the consequences are very painful and sometimes even deadly. There are other risks, too. Anything containing alcohol – hairspray, perfumes, cough medicines, mouthwash, nasal sprays, cold remedies, and so on – can cause severe reactions.'

Georgia W. from *Don't Let the Bastards Grind You Down*

Dr Niall Campbell from The Priory Hospital, Roehampton, is not too keen on prescribing medication to problem drinkers in general, but acknowledges that Antabuse can have its uses in some circumstances.

'Antabuse works by stopping alcohol being fully broken down by the liver and causing high levels of acetaldehyde in the blood stream,' he explains. 'This causes patients to feel very sick, flushed and have a headache, thus strongly associating drinking with a physically unpleasant feeling. It doesn't work specifically for cravings, but in selected cases it can be surprisingly effective and can stop cravings simply because the drinker knows they can't drink.

'It has a remarkably powerful effect in shutting those with drink problems off from the possibility of drinking, and is particularly useful when the drinker knows they have to be in social situations such as weddings or work functions, where alcohol is easily available. Ideally, you need someone supervising the drinker to make sure they are taking it.'

In *The Cure for Alcoholism*, Roy Eskapa goes so far as to describe Antabuse as being the equivalent of 'locking up a patient in a prison or mental facility where no alcohol is available'. He argues that enforced abstinence produces an alcohol deprivation effect, which increases cravings, and that animal studies have shown that Antabuse and similar medicines increase the craving even more than abstinence, meaning that people become anxious to get rid of the medication and start drinking again.

'The craving induces people to quit taking Antabuse so they can start drinking again. There are stories of alcoholics cutting open their arms or abdomens to remove slow-release capsules in order to be free to start drinking.

> Antabuse, therefore, is *not* a cure because it fails to remove the basics for alcoholism, as proven by the fact that it fails to reduce the craving. Instead, Antabuse actually leads to an increase in craving.'
>
> Roy Eskapa from *The Cure For Alcoholism*

Another frequently prescribed medication is Acamprosate (also known as Campral). This can help with cravings if taken several times a day, but alcohol experts are deeply divided over its effectiveness. Professor Roger Williams of the International Centre for Research into Liver Disorders, feels it is the first one of the pharmaceutical agents that should be tried. The Priory's Dr Niall Campbell, on the other hand, doesn't have much faith in it and Professor Keith Humphreys of Stanford University says, 'It seems to work in France, but trials outside France have been very disappointing. I don't know why.'

Naltrexone (also known as Revia) can be used to reduce cravings for those who have gone dry, although we will see in Chapter 6 that it is also being used in a completely different context, to enable those who are still drinking to revert to drinking in moderation. It is not actually licensed in the UK for combating alcohol addiction, although it can be prescribed for the purpose to specific individuals at the doctor's discretion.

Professor John Saunders at the University of Sydney says, 'Naltrexone is an evidence-based treatment and I prescribe it to approximately two thirds of my patients with alcohol dependence.'

Dr Alex Wodak at St Vincent's Hospital says, 'Naltrexone and Acamprosate achieve approximately 30 per cent abstinence at twelve months. This is double the rate seen with a placebo, and a worthwhile benefit, but not as good as seen with supervised Antabuse.'

Ultimately, the suitability or otherwise of any of these forms of medication is likely to depend on your drinker's particular situation, and the potential pros and cons should therefore be discussed with a suitable medical professional.

Detoxes and Counselling

The availability of medical detoxes, which can help the withdrawal process by administering substitute drugs in decreasing quantities over a period of days, will depend to a great extent on the country you live in, but it may well not be necessary to pay. In the UK, for example, it can be possible to have a detox free of charge at your local GP's surgery, drug and alcohol centre or even sometimes as an inpatient on the NHS. Exactly what is available will vary significantly from one part of the country to another.

It can also be possible to pay to have a detox administered in the comfort of the drinker's own home, and they may even be allowed to administer their own detox if they're deemed trustworthy and considered to have a sufficiently supportive partner or immediate family.

Undergoing a detox is only the first stage in the recovery process for someone with a physical addiction. From the point when it is completed they could require – in addition to all the support possible from those around them – both regular counselling and regular attendance at a self-help group. As with so many aspects of tackling a drink problem, finding the right therapist can involve a certain amount of trial and error, so the message is to encourage them not to give up if they don't happen to hit it off with the first one they choose.

Dr Bruce Trathen at dryoutnow.com says, 'When we get on to full-blown therapy, the most rigorous studies have failed to find any significant difference in outcomes for people, dependant on the type of therapy used. My personal view is that success or otherwise is more about the quality of interaction between the individual therapist and the individual with the problem than with the theoretical form of therapy that's used. And, anyway, in the real world there are very few "purists" out there. Most counsellors will use whatever skills they feel are appropriate to the interaction at a given point in time.'

In an ideal world the first port of call should be an addiction counsellor, but if none are available in the drinker's locality it could be worth trying a clinical psychologist, psychiatrist, psychotherapist or even a general counsellor. As long as the individual requiring counselling is abstinent at the time, it may only be necessary to attend once a week. If they are still drinking, on the other hand, they may require several sessions a week with an addiction counsellor and the costs involved with this can be so steep that it might prove better value to spend some time in a private residential rehab clinic.

Residential Rehab

Stays in residential rehab, which often include a medical detox, can last anything between four weeks and eighteen months, but most people stay somewhere between four to twelve weeks. Therapy, which usually involves plenty of group discussions as well as one-to-one sessions, aims to help the drinker understand why they drink and to develop alternatives to alcohol. Considerable emphasis is also placed on teaching coping skills to tackle cravings and to recognize and deal with other potential trigger points that could result in relapse. Drinkers may find themselves facing up to a variety of different issues, but getting it all off their chest can be a highly liberating experience.

Amanda Holland, a counsellor and psychotherapist based in Huntingdon in Cambridgeshire, who specializes in addiction, says, 'People get very honest in rehab. I have heard people talk about things they've never told anyone in their lives. Because they feel it's a safe environment, it can be very helpful in getting some of that stuff out. Some say you are as sick as your secrets.'

Rehab isn't always an appropriate solution, though, particularly if the drinker concerned doesn't need a detox and is both self-motivated and co-operative, and some experts express reservations generally about the wisdom of subjecting drinkers to an artificial environment from which they will have to subsequently readjust to the outside world.

'Celebrities who go on television after rehab with shining eyes and talk about their spiritual awakenings and new-found commitment to sobriety are not speaking falsely. They are simply describing the genuine experience they had in rehab. They have indeed found inner peace, as I had in each of my rehab stays. But it is a fragile peace, and strong emotion, positive or negative, can trigger the unrest of chronic dysphoria, and all one craves is relief from it.'

Dr Olivier Ameisen from *The End of My Addiction*

Success rates enjoyed by different rehab clinics are notoriously difficult to fathom and, whilst some claim that as many as two thirds of attendees have remained dry for twelve months after leaving, closer examination invariably finds this to be something of an exaggeration. It may well be that their own research finds two thirds of respondents to the questionnaire they sent out remained dry for twelve months, but that is quite a different matter. Someone is far less likely to respond to such a circular if they have fallen off the wagon, because their pride will be affected and they may also be concerned that knowledge of their relapse could have implications for their marriage or career.

One thing experts tend to agree on is that the longer someone spends in rehab the greater the chances of them overcoming their drink problem. Someone who has spent a month in a standard rehab clinic may therefore benefit from a further spell in second-ary rehab immediately afterwards.

Keith Burns of ADMIT Services says, 'Many clinics run a twenty-eight-day rehab programme. This can be ideal for certain categories of drinker, but the success rates are statistically much higher the longer the programme. Whether a more lengthy stay is best depends largely on the individual's age, maturity and life experience.'

Burns emphasizes that everyone is different, but usually sug-gests that younger people (those aged approximately under thirty) go in for at least eight weeks and ideally twelve, whereas older people tend to need less time and go in for perhaps four to eight weeks. He feels that effective low-cost clinics, particularly in South Africa, can be ideal for people wishing to access long-term, low-cost treatments, but that you need specialist advice to find the right place. His success rates are around 85 per cent.

▓ CASE STUDY Secondary Rehab Overseas

Exchange rate considerations have played a major part in ensuring that South Africa has been a popular destination during recent years for those requiring secondary rehab. A twelve-week stay at the Oasis rehab clinic in Plettenburg Bay can, for example, cost as little as three thousand pounds. Not surprisingly, therefore, many of its residents come from as far afield as the UK, Ireland, Italy, Portugal, Holland, Spain, the US and Canada.

Indeed, international residents typically occupy two thirds of its twelve beds at any one time, and South Africans only one third. They stay for a minimum of twelve weeks and can remain longer at Solar House, its tertiary care facility. This costs just over five hundred pounds a month and they can stay for as long as they need to. Patients, unless they are paid for by medical insurance schemes, are normally entirely privately funded, but residents are encouraged to be self-supporting and not to depend on their families.

The small size of the centre allows each client to be treated as an individual by a therapeutic team that consists of two senior and experienced psychotherapists and an addiction counsellor. All house managers are themselves addicts in recovery and are often studying to be counsellors. Based on the Minnesota Model, addiction is viewed as a disease that cannot be cured but can be treated, and the 12 Step Programme provides a means for people to take control of their own continued treatment long after they have left the confines of the clinic.

'The treatment we provide is more psychodynamic than purely 12 Step,' explains Anstice Wright, Clinical Director at Oasis. 'We aim to treat the person not the symptom, which is addiction. We are more interested in what causes the person to run away into addiction than in the addiction itself, and to do this the person needs to be dry and to begin to have more clarity about what works and what doesn't work in their life. The 12 Steps provides an excellent framework for this at the client's own pace.'

'Family members often travel from around the world to come to Plettenburg Bay for a week towards the end of the second month of their loved one's treatment.'

Living 24/7 in a family-type environment where all behaviours and possible 'dodginess' will be exposed is where the healing starts, and it becomes clear which behaviours cause the problems.

All the rooms are around a central courtyard and swimming pool and, because of the small number of residents, there isn't much opportunity for flying under the radar. A morning walk on the beach is followed at the same time every day by group therapy.

'Group is sacrosanct,' continues Wright. 'It's where the work takes place. It's where you can hear others talk about their feelings of shame or guilt and feelings of "less than", and it is the start of not being alone. Of course it's also a place where you can be confronted by your peers and counsellors on your dodgy or addictive behaviour, but this means you have to stop kidding people, and that mask of pretending to be OK and not needing any help can gradually be taken off.'

The voyage of self-discovery is aided by one-to-one counselling and Step work. The reality of discovering who one is today as opposed to who one wants to be or how one still tries to see oneself can feel very shaming, so the Oasis philosophy is that this should not be done alone. As a sense of trust develops among the group, so does a sense of spirituality and a belief that if someone can be accepted by human beings it may also be possible for them to accept a higher power.

Assignment work to fit a particular client is also done according to the traits that become obvious in this small community. It may, for example, be necessary to work on areas such as the need to control, power games, compliance versus surrender, anger, shame, masks or relationships.

'We are more interested in what causes the person to run away into addiction than in the addiction itself.'

Free time is also a challenge as it involves learning how to plan and manage time, and residents are able to participate in everything from yoga, meditation and horse riding to ocean adventures and swimming with seals or, sometimes, dolphins. There are also opportunities to visit places of outstanding beauty and spirituality and to attend an overnight camp and participate in an outward-bound experience.

The number of international residents and the fact that South Africa is a big country – so even families of native residents often live a long way away – means there are no regular family group meetings. Nevertheless, family members often travel from around the world to come to Plettenburg Bay for a week towards the end of the second month of their loved one's treatment.

If Oasis can arrange for more than one family to be present

at the same time, it will organize family groups in addition to the individual family counselling that families have, both with and without the resident. Families are able to spend time going out with the recovering addict knowing that they have a safe place to come back to if things get difficult. This seems to be beneficial and brings a touch of reality to both parties about how to move forwards in the knowledge that there is no miracle cure.

Who Should Pay?

If rehab treatment is not being funded by the state or by a company health insurance scheme, cost can obviously play a major part in determining the length of stay that's appropriate. If you have already pushed the boat out to fund a month-long stay in primary rehab for your loved one, then the mere mention of the possibility of secondary rehab can be enough to send shivers down your spine. After all, it was probably not something you had even considered when you sat down and worked out whether you could afford to pay for their rehab in the first place.

It's important to recognize, therefore, that, wherever possible, treatment of any sort should be funded from the drinker's assets rather than your own. You should not even be considering paying unless the drinker doesn't actually have any assets or is still a teenager.

If an adult needing rehab treatment has a car or flat, then the starting point is for them to sell them, because rehab is far more likely to be effective if they have paid for it. One of the reasons rehab handed out on the state tends to have disappointing results is undoubtedly because it's free.

Counsellor Amanda Holland says, 'In my experience those whose stay in rehab is being paid for by friends, relatives or insurance companies are far less likely to get well. It is therefore important that the drinkers themselves meet the costs, if they are in a position to do so, or at the very least are committed to repaying the money in the future. For example, a nineteen-year-old I worked with had sold her car in order to contribute to the cost.

'Someone truly intent on recovery will use all the personal funds they have available. They will perhaps also need contributions from others, but these others should only support the cost if they are certain in the knowledge that the person has truly given all they are able to first. By doing it this way they will be helping the one they care about.'

Instead of paying for the treatment, you can make a far more worthwhile contribution to a drinker's recovery by showing the right level of support while they are there. The first step should be to sign up for the family programme offered by the treatment centre and to make sure that attendance at the sessions is made an overwhelming priority. As well as sending out the right messages to the drinker whilst they are actually in rehab, the education and support you receive from the programme will be invaluable in helping you deal with the drinker during the early stages of their recovery once they've left rehab.

▓ CASE STUDY Family Therapy Helps With Rehab Process

After experiencing losing her husband to an alcohol-related suicide twenty-four years ago, fifty-eight-year-old Mary Livingstone had probably been confident that her family's drink problems were behind her. But two years ago she received a most unexpected overseas phone call about her eldest daughter.

Lucy, now aged thirty-three, had suffered a breakdown whilst working in Greece and, having been self-harming, was being treated in a local 12 Step-based clinic. She had been attending AA meetings regularly for five months after deciding to stop drinking, but had been coming under a great deal of stress at work. On returning briefly to England, Lucy went for a consultation at Clouds House, a rehab clinic in Salisbury, Wiltshire, and she'd been told that if she didn't start feeling better she would need to return for treatment.

Unfortunately, she had barely returned to Greece before she had downed a bottle of gin and had to be rushed to a local hospital. Mary flew out immediately and accompanied her daughter back to England, driving her to Clouds House, where she spent six weeks, followed by six months of secondary rehab in its sister organization, Hope House, in Clapham in London.

'It was suggested by a member of the Clouds House family counselling team that support for Lucy shown by her family could greatly help her recovery.'

Mary, who works in the charity sector, says, 'Prior to the last couple of years I didn't know that Lucy had any kind of drink problem and found the whole thing hard to believe. She had apparently been going to AA in Athens, but it clearly hadn't provided enough support for her on its own, and I think a lot of her problems were linked to losing her father so tragically at the age of eight.'

It was suggested by a member of the Clouds House family counselling team that support for Lucy shown by her family could greatly help her recovery, so Mary and her other daughter, thirty-one-year-old Melissa, attended a couple of family therapy sessions with Lucy on Sunday afternoons at Clouds House, and a further session at Hope House. The first session at Clouds, which took place on Mothering Sunday, proved as beneficial as it was harrowing.

'It was excellent because it was an opportunity to be honest,' explains Mary. 'We all thought we were very close, but we had always deflected the truth and skimmed over the surface emotionally. My two daughters, for example, spelled out the fact that my level of anger was uncontrollable when they were tiny. In the Hope House session Lucy even told me in front of two counsellors to "cut the crap, Mum, I was there", which made me realize that she hadn't been deceived about how grim it all was.

'These types of sessions are essential as far as I'm concerned. They are painful and hard but they are certainly worth it, because we are much more honest with each other now and the elephant in the room has shrunk to a much smaller size – you can actually see around it!'

'We all thought we were very close, but we had always deflected the truth and skimmed over the surface emotionally.'

After leaving Hope House, Lucy attended AA in England for three months and, whilst her mother was happy to drive her to meetings when asked to, she took great care not to be seen to be acting as a form of policing mechanism. Lucy then returned to Greece, where she is still well, sober and regularly attending AA. In December 2010 she visited England for what Mary describes as a 'wonderful family Christmas'. With no alcohol present at all for the first festive season ever, everyone was able to enjoy a very happy time together at the church, followed by a walk and playing games.

'By helping Lucy I ended up helping myself far more than I expected,' reveals Mary. 'Both Melissa and myself started having individual counselling sessions at the time that Lucy came back to England to attend Clouds House, and I also went on a five-day Families Plus therapeutic programme affili-ated to Clouds, which proved extremely beneficial. Most of the pain I went through during the course related to the time when my husband was ill and the period after his death, as opposed to my daughter, and twenty-four years later it was definitely still worth doing. I was finally able to be totally honest about what I've lived through and to realize that it's not my fault.'

In summary

- We urge you not to give up just because one or two forms of treatment don't work, and not to rule out a form of treatment just because another practitioner writes it off

- Simply introducing someone to AA can change their lives, as can informing them that their doctor can prescribe medication to deter them from touching alcohol or to reduce cravings

- Remember that, wherever possible, private treatment for adult drinkers should be paid for from the drinker's own assets

- Make sure you join in the family programme offered by the rehab clinic the drinker is attending

CHAPTER SIX

Newer and Less Conventional Methods of Treatment

There are obvious risks in using any method that hasn't yet built up the type of track record and credibility – via clinical trials – that leading addiction experts like to see before recommending it. Nevertheless, if someone is clearly going to die unless they find an effective form of treatment for their drinking problem there can be an equally compelling case for throwing caution to the wind.

We would like to stress that those who promote the methods we look at in this chapter believe they are commendably safe. Nevertheless, a further medical opinion is obviously advisable and ongoing research can throw up surprising results that may suggest a new method should be considered in a dramatically new light, either positive or negative. We therefore strongly advise that these approaches are only considered in conjunction with appropriate medical advice.

We also recommend that anyone interested in these methods should keep their eyes and ears open for updates on their progress by reading the health sections in newspapers, conducting online searches and chatting to the other families, friends and partners of problem drinkers who they might meet at self-help groups or at the family sessions at rehab clinics.

It is even possible that further exciting new forms of treatment may become available at some point in the future, so being aware is all important. In fact, we ourselves found out about some of these newer methods via the Internet two years ago by simply typing the words, 'cure for alcoholism' into a search engine, and then proceeded to do as much research as we could, including speaking to those who had developed the methods.

These newer methods in our view give real hope to even the most chronic cases. But the fact remains that the majority of those with drink problems – and those who love them most – are still unaware of the existence of these approaches, so simply bringing them to their attention could turn out to be the greatest gift you ever gave them. Whether the drinker actually goes ahead with treatment, however – like all other decisions involved with their recovery, whatever the method used – is ultimately their call.

We urge you not to be put off by any negative comments you might hear from traditional practitioners who have never seriously considered these newer methods. After all, it's not as though the traditional approaches don't have their fair share of critics as well and, whilst they have done, and continue to do, good for millions of people, their users have significant relapse rates, which highlights the fact that there is no one-size-fits-all approach.

One common reservation about some of the newer methods expressed by those who work in rehab centres is that they effectively replace one form of dependence with another. But once again we reiterate our view that it is surely better to be dependent on something that enables you to function and lead a reasonably normal life than on something that doesn't. After all, most of us are dependent on one thing or another to help us get through life.

I (Edmund Tirbutt) am the first to admit that I'm addicted to work, exercise and occasional binge eating, and that I'm aware of the risks associated with overdoing any one of these. Nevertheless, my life is immeasurably happier and more productive than in the days when I was drinking. Similarly, a common criticism levelled at those who attend AA is that they have swapped an obsession with alcohol for an obsession with AA, but it doesn't take a genius to work out which obsession is healthier!

As far as we are concerned, any method of combating alcohol addiction that has worked for one person could also work for others and should not be ruled out. So your bunch of keys could include anything from AA or other self-help group meetings, residential rehab and counselling to hypnosis, acupuncture, cognitive behavioural therapy (CBT), yoga and meditation. We also think it should include the newer methods we discuss below.

We would like to highlight four methods that we feel have shown exceptional potential and exciting results. All are obviously controversial, in the sense that they claim to enable someone with a physical addiction to go back to drinking in moderation and, as we have seen in Chapter 2, the conventional wisdom is that those who have been physically addicted should never touch another drop for as long as they live.

The Ameisen Baclofen Programme

One hugely exciting recent development has been the realization that baclofen, a drug that had already been around as a muscle relaxant for some fifty years, can enable those with physical addictions to be cured both from cravings and from the addiction itself – allowing them even to go back to drinking again in moderation. The discovery of baclofen as a cure for alcoholism was made by Professor Olivier Ameisen, a French-American cardiologist, who had had a serious drink problem and suffered from terrible cravings linked to severe anxiety problems.

Ameisen found that conventional methods like AA and rehab did not prevent him from relapsing. However, a newspaper article he read in 2000 about how a University of Pennsylvania researcher was studying the effects of baclofen on drug addicts' craving for cocaine sowed the seeds of the idea that led to his discovery and cure.

By starting on very low dosages of baclofen and gradually increasing them, Professor Ameisen soon found that he was achieving remarkable short-term results. Within the first few days he felt that his muscles were completely relaxed, that he could at long last sleep peacefully and that his anxiety was far more under control than it had been using any standard medications. At 180mg per day the drug limited the extent of his binges, reducing his cravings and enabling him to remain abstinent for longer periods between binges.

'Craving for an addictive substance, or a compulsive behaviour, is the primary symptom of addiction and compulsion in two senses. From the suffering patient's point of view, craving is the constant enemy that must be battled – even after years of abstinence. And from the point of view of the disease process, craving is now recognized as the number-one cause of relapse.'

Dr Olivier Ameisen from *The End of My Addiction*

He realized that animals completely lost their urge to drink at higher dosages of baclofen, so he decided to increase the dose in the hope that it could suppress his craving. By the time he had reached his personal 'tip-over point' at 270mg a day, he found that he felt no desire to drink alcohol whilst in the company of people drinking, which had never previously been the case during a lifetime of alcohol abuse. He felt that his brain had effectively reverted to the state it was in before he developed a drink problem.

On rare occasions since then he has had a glass or two of champagne, vodka and tonic or gin and tonic at gatherings with friends, but he has basically completely lost the desire to drink and barely ever drinks at all.

Once he published his book *The End of My Addiction*, and the approach started being used by other people, it became obvious that baclofen reversed the process of alcoholism for others, too, and that the cure was dose-dependent; i.e., those adopting the Ameisen Baclofen Programme used different levels of baclofen to reach their personal tipping points. In some cases a dose of 90mg per day can be sufficient to cure someone, but in other cases up to 300 or 400mg may be required, or even higher in some rare instances.

There can be a number of reasons for this large dose differential, but the levels of underlying anxiety an individual suffers from can be a key indicator of what level of baclofen is needed. It can take many months of gradually increasing the dosage to find the right level and keep it there for a period of time – which, again, can vary – but, once there, the results can be staggering.

When someone finds the right level of baclofen which 'tips them over' into a non-addictive state, it is also known as 'the switch' as it literally switches the brain chemistry from being addicted to non-addicted to alcohol.

However, the key point to note is that the cure is dose-dependent. For some, as in the case of Professor Ameisen himself, results can be immediate. He lost his desire to drink alcohol the first day he took his dose from 250 to 270mgs. For others the tip-over, or switch, can be more gradual. The key is to keep on trying to find the dose at which a drinker tips over and to maintain this dose for a period of time.

A key question asked is when will a drinker know they have tipped over? Essentially, the switch happens when the person with the serious addiction loses any desire to drink alcohol – which, according to more conventional methods, is a miracle for a physically addicted drinker – and is literally indifferent to it. In the case of Professor Ameisen, he recalls how, after feeling neutral to those drinking around him, he looked at the bar and the 'bottles no longer called out his name'.

There have already been over 600 documented cases worldwide in the hands of academic physicians, both in the US and Europe, of alcoholic patients who have been entirely disease-free – some for as long as four and a half years – as a result of using the Ameisen Baclofen Programme. Additionally, Professor Ameisen, who was made visiting Professor of Medicine at the State University of New York Downstate Medical Center in 2008 in acknowledgement of his discovery, also receives around ten emails a day from patients or their relatives, expressing eternal gratitude for the fact that they, or their loved ones, have been cured.

Because baclofen makes them feel good, there is rarely a problem getting people to take their pills, and Professor Ameisen and Dr de Beaurepaire recently published a paper in a medical journal that demonstrates that the baclofen programme completely supresses alcohol addiction in 88 per cent of patients. Roughly half of these stop drinking completely, whilst the remainder carry on drinking occasionally, but in a perfectly controlled fashion. Professor Ameisen emphasizes that the drug gives you a feeling of wellbeing that makes drink irrelevant, which is completely different from abstinence, and that it can cure the underlying problems that made the individual turn to drink in the first place. So, unlike many other methods, it can provide a total cure.

It should, however, be noted that people should start this programme in conjunction with their GP. Also, after a tip-over, baclofen doses should be slowly reduced. As with many other medications, such as tranquillizers or blood pressure treatments, it is recommended that in the first weeks of treatment the person on baclofen should not drive and should, as with any chronic disease, carry a card saying how much baclofen they are taking in case of an unrelated emergency.

'Baclofen is the best hope for addiction treatment, and all the available data indicates that it is as safe for long-term use as it is effective. There is not one report of a severe side effect that didn't revert, compared to many deaths caused by aspirin and paracetamol which can be bought over the counter,' explains Professor Ameisen.

'If one accepts that alcoholism kills more patients a day than any one form of cancer, one would drop silly questions such as putative side effects that have never taken place in its half century of use. If we learned today that baclofen cured patients from pancreatic cancer worldwide, every doctor in his right mind would rush to prescribe it without the slightest hesitation. Do alcoholics not deserve the same right to live?'

Professor Ameisen also recommends that the patient should take, in addition to baclofen, vitamin B1 every day. Chronic drinkers often suffer from B1 deficiency due to, amongst other things, inadequate nutritional intake. Nerve cells and other supporting cells require B1, and a lack of this vitamin in the system can result in a number of neurological disorders.

Despite the early success of baclofen for the treatment and cure of alcoholism and the underlying anxiety that can cause it, Professor Ameisen acknowledges that two potentially limiting side effects of high doses of baclofen are drowsiness and muscular weakness. But these usually last at most a day or two and are always completely reversible once the body adjusts to the new levels of baclofen in the system. He personally experienced inconvenient drowsiness when taking 270mg of baclofen a day, but the effects rapidly disappeared at a lower dose.

Ninety per cent of GPs in France now prescribe baclofen to patients with drink problems, and in the US the approach is becoming so widely recognized that people are even starting to take legal action against doctors in cases where they haven't recommended it and the patient has subsequently died. In the US, Ameisen is invited to give inaugural lectures in major universities everywhere, including at Harvard, and is received most enthusiastically. In the UK, however, many GPs have still not heard of the possibility of using baclofen in this way.

Persuading a GP to prescribe the doses necessary to reach the particular drinker's tipping point may not therefore be plain sailing. Some GPs will not feel comfortable prescribing above 100mg a day, but this level could have a very limited effect – or no effect at all – on reducing many drinkers' cravings and providing a cure. Indeed, Professor Ameisen expresses frustration at the fact that some clinical trials taking place only involve a dose of 100mg per day, as they are most unlikely to reflect the true potential benefits of baclofen in their results.

The best method of persuading a doctor to consider using baclofen for this purpose is to take them a copy of Professor Olivier Amesien's book *The End of My Addiction*, published by Piatkus in the UK; Farrar, Straus and Giroux in the US; Denoël in France; Kuntsmann in Germany; Nieuwezijds in the Netherlands; Objetiva in Brazil and Baldini Castoldi in Italy.

It should be noted that the title Professor Ameisen uses as author of the book is 'Dr Olivier Ameisen'.

▓ CASE STUDY Patience With Baclofen Pays Off Eventually

Fifty-one-year-old Noni Thiesen admits that she still sometimes has to pinch herself to confirm that it's all really happening. For the last four and half years she has been living life to the full without touching a drop of alcohol or feeling any temptation to do so. For the previous thirty years, she had been fighting a seemingly losing battle against a highly destructive drink problem that had seen her fired from half a dozen jobs and become pretty much written off by half of her ten brothers and sisters.

'I was either going to die by my own hand or the alcohol was going to kill me,' she admits. 'I used to get these terrible cravings triggered by anxiety attacks and they were so all-consuming that logic seemed to fly out of the window at the time. I became a walking shell of a human being who rarely left the house except to get booze, and there were days when I could only get out of bed to puke. On other days, when I couldn't get out of bed, I would keep a pan beside me.

'The longest I managed to remain sober for was for ten months, and I was in a rehab clinic for six months of that time. I had tried five stays in rehab in total and was in and out of AA for some twenty years. I had sought help from a range of different clergy and had tried counselling and even acupuncture. In fact, I'd tried everything I could think of.'

Then one evening in 2004, her life changed completely when her long-suffering husband, Randy, was surfing the Internet and came across a paper in the medical Journal *Alcohol and Alcoholism*, in which Professor Olivier Ameisen had reported how he cured himself of what seemed like a similar problem to Noni's by using baclofen.

'He always used to say that he knew the real Noni was in there somewhere and that one day he was going to get her back.'

The timing of the discovery could not have been better, because the very next day Noni had an appointment with a neurologist in her home town of Kalispell, Montana, in the US. In what seemed to her like a final throw of the dice, she had arranged an appointment six weeks earlier to see if there might be any new treatments for alcohol addiction that he had heard of.

'As soon as I read the story of Professor Ameisen's that Randy had printed off for me I thought, 'This is me', and took it to the neurologist, asking him if he could prescribe baclofen. Initially he was sceptical, as he knew the drug only as a muscle relaxant, but I begged him to help me and he agreed to try a small dose and to work from there.'

The first dose was only 30mg a day and, although this helped reduce her cravings, it did not prevent her from relapsing. The therapist she was seeing at the time advised her to ask the doctor to increase the dosage, because she noticed that Ameisen had written that the effects of baclofen were dose-dependent. He agreed to do so gradually and, despite two further relapses over the next eighteen months, Noni finally arrived at what was clearly her 'tipping point' at 180mgs a day. By holding the dosage at this level for three months she got rid of all her cravings completely and effort-lessly, and having continued since then on a reduced dosage of 60mg a day, no cravings have returned.

Noni, who currently works as a garden centre caretaker and has two grown-up sons, says, 'Even though I understand that I could go back to drinking in moderation, I don't want to do so. I am so ashamed of what that substance did to me that I don't want a drop of it to ever pass my lips again. My family were obviously disappointed in me and my parents, unfortunately, died before they had the chance to see me recover.

> 'I now just take three 20mg pills a day
> and never get any cravings.
> It's really as simple as that!'

'If Randy hadn't stuck by me I don't think I would have survived, as I only had two friends left. Randy always supported me and helped to pay for my counselling sessions and rehab stays; he always used to say that he knew the real Noni was in there somewhere and that one day he was going to get her back. I now take just three 20mg pills a day and never get any cravings. It's really as simple as that!

'My message to anyone who knows a drinker is that if they are serious about trying to help them get their life back, they can succeed. As a young woman I was a happy, outgoing, athletic girl with a real zeal for what life was offering me; there was nothing I wouldn't try or do. The alcohol was very deceiving and before I knew it I couldn't seem to live without it, but I now have that young woman's energy back and I wouldn't trade it for anything.

'The drinker has nothing to lose by trying this approach, so try and persuade them to give themselves a chance,' she continues. 'Get them to find a physician who will support them and try and find the right dosage. Different people require different dosages and it may take many months to find the right one.'

The Sinclair Method

We have seen in Chapter 5 (page 137) how naltrexone is a mainstream medication prescribed – albeit with modest success – for those who have already gone through detox to try and help reduce their cravings. The Sinclair Method uses naltrexone in a different context as there is no prior detoxification. The drinker caries on drinking, but takes naltrexone an hour before drinking, and each time this is done the craving is reduced one step lower by a mechanism called 'extinction', thus control over drinking is gradually regained. Clinical trials and normal clinical practice have shown that naltrexone can have a remarkable effect when used in this way.

'The Sinclair Method is easier than dieting because you do not have to avoid the temptation to drink. Naltrexone + Drinking works automatically – it is your formula for successful de-addiction.'

Roy Eskapa from *The Cure for Alcoholism*

When you consume sugar, saccharin and alcohol you cause endorphins to be released in the brain, but naltrexone has the ability to block the effect of these endorphins. Every time someone has a drink while naltrexone is in the bloodstream they will weaken the endorphin-reinforced pathways that have become hardwired into the brain in a way that controls the sufferer's drinking.

Taking naltrexone an hour before drinking progressively reverses this addiction. Benefits can be seen as soon as ten days after first use, but the effects become several times stronger after three or four months. By this point the drinker has ceased to be obsessed with alcohol and the benefits continue indefinitely as long as they continue to take naltrexone when they drink. Some choose to carry on drinking at safe and controllable levels, whilst others decide to quit drinking altogether.

Dr David Sinclair, the pioneer of the method who works as a researcher at the National Institute for Health and Welfare in Finland, refers to 78 per cent or even higher success rates from use in clinics and feels that the approach, which has successfully cured an estimated 70,000 patients in Finland since the early 1990s, is especially commendable for being safe, cheap and humane, and for curing alcohol addiction by restoring the brain to a condition in which cravings and interest in alcohol are similar to the way they were before the drink problem developed.

He emphasizes that the Sinclair Method can be started immediately, does not require a medical detox or inpatient treatment, works first time around and benefits those who simply want to reduce the amount they drink on certain occasions, as well as those with serious drink problems. Side effects are also regarded as less of an issue than critics make out, although he goes to great lengths to flag up the fact that the approach should not be used by addicts who are physiologically dependent upon heroin, morphine, methadone or synthetic opiates like OxyContin as naltrexone could prove fatal for them. Pregnant women are also advised not to use it.

Dr Sinclair says, 'Naltrexone in doses over 300mg has been reported to cause liver damage, but this is higher than the 50mg usually used for treating alcoholism via the Sinclair Method. There are, however, worries about giving it to patients who already have liver damage, so it's advised that patients should first have a blood sample taken and analysed for liver damage. Interestingly, one of the primary findings of clinical trials, including our own, has been a significant improvement in the measures of liver damage. In other words, the reduction of drinking is far more beneficial to the liver than any harm caused by naltrexone.'

Around 10 to 20 per cent of patients report nausea or intestinal upset when they first start using naltrexone, but the effects are usually small. However, one side effect Dr Sinclair had predicted, and which was reported in several trials, is the weakening of other behaviours that are reinforced by endorphins, such as eating sweets, sex and exercise. So a method called selective extinction has been developed in order to avoid this problem and, indeed, actually taking advantage of it. Basically, it consists of avoiding those healthy behaviours on days when taking naltrexone, but practising them when the medication has cleared the system.

'If you are a patient following the Sinclair Method you have only one absolute rule: take naltrexone before drinking. You must take your medication for the rest of your life – but only when you drink alcohol.'

Roy Eskapa from *The Cure For Alcoholism*

One potential downside of the Sinclair Method that's commonly highlighted is that it will only work if those with a drink problem take their medication. However, compliance is reported to be extraordinarily good at 85 per cent. Those who want to regain control of their drinking have little difficulty remembering to take a pill before they start to drink; what is hard for them is avoiding drinking, which is what most other treatments require. Probably of greater concern is the fact that it can be hard to find a doctor outside Finland who is willing to prescribe naltrexone in this way.

Naltrexone has been approved for alcoholism in the US since 1995 and in more than a dozen other countries since then. But even if you live in a country such as the UK, where it is not licensed for alcohol addiction, it doesn't mean that the Sinclair Method cannot be used. Naltrexone itself has been

approved as a medicine in nearly all countries and can be prescribed to an individual at a doctor's discretion. GPs can
understandably be reluctant to prescribe something for a
purpose they are not familiar with but, if they have been
working with the drinker and using other methods that have
failed to work, they may be open to new ideas. A good way of
broaching the subject initially would be to show them the letter
composed by Dr David Sinclair on the page overleaf, then possibly leave them a copy of Roy Eskapa's book *The Cure For
Alcoholism* to read.

■ CASE STUDY 'Magical Cure' Works for Seemingly Hopeless Case

International sales rep Patricia Hodgson struggles to count
the number of different methods she has tried for combating
her drink problem on the fingers of both hands. From AA to
prescribed medication, nothing seemed to work.

A course of Antabuse (see Chapter 5, page 135) was
shelved after a couple of months because, knowing it would
make her violently sick if she subsequently drank, she
simply didn't take her pills. A month in rehab was considered a 'waste of time and money', and seeing a therapist for
a year, whilst certainly helping her put up boundaries and
deal with issues with family and friends, did nothing to
reduce her drinking.

Patricia, who is forty-three and lives in San Diego in the
US, now drinks in moderation without having to exercise any
self-control thanks to the Sinclair Method, which she discovered a year ago. She simply takes a 50mg pill of naltrexone
an hour before drinking alcohol and tends to never want
more than a couple of glasses of wine. She experiences no side
effects at all, and when she doesn't drink she doesn't need to
take any pills.

For anyone who doubts that there can be such a seemingly magical cure for a friend or loved one, her message is quite simple: get them to try it out and see for themselves.

'In my opinion it's only a matter of time before this catches on worldwide,' she enthuses. 'It simply has to because it works for most people, has no apparent side effects and is inexpensive. It only costs me ten US dollars for thirty pills, which is almost nothing.

'Research shows that it works for over three quarters of the people who try it, which is staggering, and you don't even need to detox. I believe the Sinclair Method puts your brain back to the way it was before your problem drinking began. It just removes the compulsion.

> 'In my opinion it's only a matter of time before this catches on worldwide.'

'I wish people wouldn't be so prejudiced against something just because it's new and involves carrying on drinking,' she continues. 'AA and all these other groups have put it into peoples' minds that abstinence is the only way, but the Sinclair Method literally saved my life and the lives of two other guys I know through online chat rooms.

'To be free from such a terrible condition and from the idea that I could never drink again is indescribable. I so much wanted to feel normal, to socialize and have the odd glass of good wine with a meal. Originally I could only have a dinner party if I invited sober friends who didn't drink, and I got sick of explaining myself, particularly when I was in England. I would often make out that I was on antibiotics; I even said I was pregnant once just to get someone off my back.'

Information for Prescribing Naltrexone
(reproduced with permission)

Dear Doctor,

The patient carrying this letter to you would like to have a prescription for naltrexone. Naltrexone was approved by the FDA in 1995 for use in the treatment of alcohol dependence. Important new information has been obtained since then about how to use naltrexone.

First, a dual double-blind clinical trial showed that the usual protocol of having patients take naltrexone while abstinent is not effective. Instead, naltrexone must be taken just before drinking. Prior detoxification should be omitted; naltrexone is taken by patients who are still drinking. The resulting mechanism of extinction then gradually reduces craving and drinking over several weeks and provides a gradual detoxification. The result has been replicated and is consistent with findings from nearly all of the eighty-two clinical trials conducted to date.

Second, it is now clear that naltrexone can be prescribed by doctors without an accompanying programme of intensive counselling. Naltrexone was originally approved by the FDA as an adjunct within comprehensive programmes of alcoholism treatment. The results of Project Combine, the largest clinical trial in the alcohol field, showed that naltrexone was effective without intensive counselling and with only medical supervision similar to that which can be provided by general practitioners. The trial also showed that patients with a particular genetic marker respond especially well to naltrexone.

Third, a way has recently been developed not only to prevent inadvertent extinction of alternative healthy behaviours, but even to strengthen them. This helps to fill the vacuum as alcohol-related behaviours are extinguished.

Further detailed information can be found in Dr Roy Eskapa's book, **The Cure for Alcoholism,** Chapter 10, which contains instructions to physicians that can be downloaded for free at http://www.benbellabooks.com/cureforalcoholism/downloads/CureforAlcoholism-Ch17.pdf

David Sinclair PhD

National Institute for Health and Welfare (THL) Helsinki, Finland

Stephen Cox, MD

Head of the National Anxiety Association, University of Kentucky, Lexington, KY

'For anyone who doubts that there can be
such a seemingly magical cure for a friend or
loved one, her message is quite simple: get
them to try it and see for themselves.'

Although she had sometimes managed periods of sobriety of between three and nine months, Patricia's drinking had spiralled completely out of control by the age of thirty-eight, in response to a combination of personal issues, including relationship breakdowns and bereavements. She never seemed to be able to drink less than a bottle and a half of wine a night, and by the age of forty she was occasionally drinking a bottle of vodka a day, and would carry on drinking until she passed out. Eventually she even had to sell her house to clear off her debts.

Patricia, who met her current partner, Paul, two years ago when her drink problem was at its peak, now rarely drinks during the week, and at weekends she often leaves glasses of wine half empty at dinner parties. She has only forgotten to take her naltrexone once, and on that occasion she took it while she was drinking rather than an hour beforehand. Consequently she ended up drinking heavily that night, but she then ensured she got things back to normal the next day by taking her pill at 6 p.m. and drinking an hour later. There were no long-term repercussions.

The 101 Program

Also producing staggering results is a dietary approach to alcohol addiction called The 101 Program, devised by Genita Petralli, who has clinics in both Costa Rica and Malibu, California, in the US. It is quite possible to do her programme without attending her clinics, though. All you need is a copy of her self-published book *Alcoholism:*

The Cause & the Cure, which can be ordered from Amazon, and access to a bio-chemist who specializes in neuro-endocrinology. (Ask at the endocrinology departments at local hospitals.)

Petralli refers to success rates as high as 92 per cent for those who stay with her programme for the necessary length of time and emphasizes that the 8 per cent who relapse tend to get back in control again very quickly. She also stresses that those who successfully complete the programme enjoy advantages far beyond overcoming their drink problem. They become healthy and happy and go on to live enriched, productive, full and inspired lives.

> 'When people in this state are given the solution they need – one that works, one that they have searched for in quiet desperation for years – their lives become recharged, and in heart and soul they become like kids again. It is truly like watching someone falling in love: only they are falling in love with life.'
>
> Genita Petralli from Alcoholism: *The Cause & the Cure*

It should be stressed that completing the programme is no walk in the park. It requires considerable application and discipline over a significant period of time and those who take part should consult a qualified health professional, preferably one disciplined in naturopathy or orthomolecular medicine.

Most participants lose cravings to drink within a week and none have been known to crave alcohol by the end of the eighth week of the programme, but this is only the beginning. After the detox phase, participants enter The Ark module of the programme, which can last for between ten and eighteen months, depending on the extent of the damage that has been caused by the alcohol abuse. This module aims to heal damage done to the body or mind and to change the drinker's metabolism from one predisposed to addiction to one that is healthy. When it has been completed it is time to enter the final maintenance programme, called the Preserve and Protect phase.

Many former problem drinkers continue to drink safely and occasionally in moderation, even if they formerly had a physical addiction to alcohol. Some, however, feel so healthy they never want to drink again, even if they originally embarked on the programme with the aim of doing so.

Petralli warns, 'If alcohol has become a permanent negative feature because, for example, you have ruined your family or killed someone while drink driving, then there is much to be said for remaining dry for a lifetime. In these cases the impact of the negative relationship with alcohol is permanent and will always have an unhealthy effect on you.'

The 101 Program offers a choice of being done either as a comprehensive services package (outpatient), as an inpatient at The Biosanctuary at the Shangri-La Green Health Care Institute, or simply by using the book, without the benefits of laboratory testing, nutritional and programme counselling and personalized therapeutic nutritional therapy.

The core principle behind the approach is that you cure addiction by curing the underlying root cause, which is essentially nutrient deficiency that makes it impossible for the body and brain to naturally produce the chemicals you seek in alcohol. A search is made to find which nutrients are lacking in the drinker's body and this search can involve a certain amount of trial and error.

Five primary influences are considered to encourage either the health or the disease of an individual's cells. These are: nutrition, emotion, thought, toxicity and EMF (Electro-Magnetic Frequencies). The 101 Program addresses all of these with a holistic approach, healing the participant, breaking the addiction, correcting their brain chemistry and giving them back the choice of whether or not they drink alcohol.

Genita Petralli, who is an avid opponent of using drugs to combat alcohol addiction, explains that she kept the programme within the rules of science and documented the progression of alcohol addiction and why people are attracted to it. She found that there is a physical underlying cause to every mental health disorder and that if your body is unable to take care of itself, it will seek help externally, which will lead to the compulsiveness that is the parent of addiction.

She says, 'For too long healthcare professionals have unsuccessfully tried to diagnose and treat the symptoms of alcoholism rather than the damage that creates the symptoms. Paying a therapist $125 an hour to look for and find the dog that bit a recovering drinker when they were seven is not going to do much to stop them craving alcohol or relieve them of chemical depression. Conventional therapy models designed for addiction treatment can in fact make life more unbearable for the alcohol-depressed frame of mind. It sets the drinker on a path that focuses on negative feelings and issues, while at the same time wrestling with the painful physical and emotional symptoms of unhealthy brain chemistry.

'Talk-therapy cannot effectively address chemical addiction, nor cure it,' she continues, 'but if you feel that you need it, even after the body is healed from alcohol addiction, then you should seek it, because there are circumstances when it can be genuinely helpful. I simply first suggest getting rid of the chemical depression, craving and anxiety to see what, if anything, is still causing mental health issues. Over 85 per cent of my patients feel that life is entirely manageable without continued talk therapy. It simply begins to fall into place with a healthy body and mind at the helm of the ship once again.'

'I am utterly convinced that the propensity to become addicted to alcohol stems from a metabolic disorder caused by the initial symptoms in the person – the symptoms that encourage them to turn to alcohol in the attempt to self-treat their condition. Alcoholism is a syndrome for which we do not know all the generating biochemical abnormalities, although we are getting much closer.'

Dr Abram Hoffer from his foreword to Genita Petralli's
Alcoholism: The Cause & the Cure.

Petralli maintains that once the addiction has been achieved, a road has been paved in the biochemistry that creates cravings for products that will provide relief from their symptoms and that, until the addictive biochemistry is completely healed, use of products such as sugar and caffeine can open the gates to those roads again and derail progress. In order to achieve true health and freedom from addiction, addicts must completely avoid commonplace food items that encourage addictive biochemistry. She says that around 90 per cent of what is sold in our supermarkets as food is the type of lifeless, refined carbs that underwrite addiction by setting the stage for it in our biochemistry at an early age.

'Addiction to any substance affects every aspect of our lives,' she continues. 'You cannot harm or heal one aspect of your life without it affecting all others. So long as they are fighting their cravings from addiction, the symptoms that brought them to it and the damage the addiction caused, they will be struggling with the very core of their survival system. The 101 Program cancels the symptoms by healing the mind and body.'

▦ CASE STUDY The 101 Program Opens Up a Whole New Way of Life

As a high-flying executive in the technology field, few who knew fifty-five-year-old Carol Coats had any inkling that she was drinking uncontrollably from dawn to dusk every day. But by the time she underwent The 101 Program in 2004, her addiction dated back twenty years and had benefited little from AA, inpatient and outpatient programmes, counselling or a variety of medications, including Antabuse.

'Prescription and over-the-counter drugs had become a way of life to combat hangovers and tiredness, and I was convinced that this was going to be the way it was until I died,' explains Carol, who lives in Virginia, in the US, with her husband and two teenage children. 'I held down my job and had a wonderful family, but I simply couldn't function without alcohol. Since going on The 101 Program, however, I have not only been dry but, most importantly, I no longer constantly crave alcohol. This is because the programme has addressed the biochemical imbalance in my brain.

'It was hard at first, but not as hard as the other programmes I have been on. It adjusts your biochemistry and for a week I didn't feel great, but that soon passed. I then began doing things I hadn't been able to do in twenty years, such as taking long walks with my family and rejoining the gym. It has been truly amazing. The programme is not just about the absence of alcohol, it's about the presence of health. If you genuinely want to become wholesome and healthy and regain the joy that alcohol takes from all of us, then this is the way to do it.'

'Most importantly I no longer constantly crave alcohol. This is because the programme has addressed the biochemical imbalance in my brain.'

After contacting Genita Petralli online and expressing a desire to sign up for The 101 Program as an outpatient, Carol was invited to fax detailed information about her nutritional intake. Once this had been assessed by Petralli, she received an appropriate package of supplements to meet her individual needs. She was then required to begin a two-month detox period, which involved consuming no meat, dairy products, processed foods, caffeine, sugar or gluten.

During the eighth week of the detox, after her intake of supplements had been suspended for a week, she was required to turn up at a local hospital to provide blood, urine and saliva samples. Based on laboratory tests performed on these, Genita Petralli developed a specific biochemical formula for Carol, who was a classic case of someone with low blood sugar levels and adrenal fatigue and, as is common with drinkers, low levels of serotonin.

The recommendations formed the basis of her treatment programme for the next nine months. At no point, during either the detox or the Ark module, did she have to take any time off work. Indeed, from a very early stage it helped her performance in the workplace, and colleagues frequently commented that she seemed much more vibrant and alert.

> 'The rewards start kicking in very quickly, so you don't feel tempted to drop out once you have started the programme.'

'It's not about giving something up but about adopting something new,' explains Carol, 'and the rewards start kicking in very quickly so you don't feel tempted to drop out once you have started the programme. It has given me my life back, and within six months of completing the course I had paid a visit to Mexico, where I was supposed to have been designing a home for the past twenty years but had never actually got around to it. I am now able to enjoy family life far more and do things like attend school functions. My family are absolutely delighted.'

Carol's father, who'd had chronic alcohol problems of his own, was so impressed by the effect it had on his daughter that he decided to undergo The 101 Program himself at the age of eighty-two. His resulting recovery enabled Carol to spend what she describes as 'five beautiful years' with him before he passed away recently.

Neurofeedback

Another method that claims to enable some of those with physical addictions to go back to drinking in moderation is Neurofeedback, which essentially involves exercising the brain. Those involved with pioneering the approach are the first to admit that they don't have sufficiently robust evidence to prove this. For the time being, Neurofeedback is rarely employed as a stand-alone technique when dealing with addiction, but it can reduce or replace the need for medication and lead to a deeper level of engagement with therapists.

Neurofeedback can also be used to good effect by the friends and loved ones of drinkers, as well as by the drinkers themselves, and the approach is taking off in the US, Netherlands, Czech Republic, Switzerland, Germany, Norway, Australia and Canada.

Jeffrey Huttman at Challenges says, 'There has been extensive research involving Neurofeedback, which has produced evidence of significant improvement in the recovery rates of individuals going through a complete cycle in conjunction with other common treatment practices for addiction. Neurofeedback is a cutting-edge strategy that is useful for optimizing the arousal levels of individuals who complete a course of treatment. In very general terms, this approach often allows those receiving addiction treatment to stabilize their brain and think more clearly, which better enables them to absorb treatment and practise recovery strategies.'

Neurofeedback, which is also called EEG biofeedback, observes your brain in action from moment to moment by monitoring brain waves. Participants are shown their brain activity and helped to change it by rewarding shifts towards a more appropriate and stable brain state. The 'electroencephalogram' (EEG) is another name for the brainwave recordings, and biofeedback refers to the process by which you learn to change your brain waves and therefore gain better control over brain status.

It targets the 'bioelectrical' functioning of the brain, which is considered more directly relevant than the chemical imbalances that are more often talked about. Sensors are attached to the scalp with EEG paste and these pick up brainwaves without causing any pain or sending any voltage or current to the brain. A computer processes the brain waves and extracts certain information from them, which is shown to the participant in the form of a video game. The participant is then instructed how to play the video game using only their brain waves.

Siegfried Othmer, Chief Scientist at the EEG Institute based in Woodland Hills in California, USA, maintains that addictions accrue from both psychological and physiological factors, and the prevailing remedies predominantly appeal to one of these domains. Targeting either of these domains selectively has not, however, had good clinical outcomes, especially in the long run. This is because the realm that connects the domain of physiology with that of psychodynamics has been oddly missing from theory and practice.

This is the realm of brain behaviour, or that which overtly organizes a person's state from moment to moment. Through Neurofeedback one is able to relieve the misery of addiction through understanding brain function and modifying it using its own mechanisms. It is truly new ground.

'Compared with conventional treatment, Neurofeedback clearly fares better with the more intractable cases of addiction,' explains Othmer, 'but the addiction community is not broad-minded enough and tends to pigeonhole this technique for things other than addiction. The more intractable cases involve more complex issues than just chemical dependency. Neurofeedback training can influence and modify these accompanying dysfunctions as well because each is governed by particular and accessible brain networks. Cases of dual diagnosis are thus broadly as addressable as straightforward cases of dependency.'

The essential challenge is to restore relevant brain networks to a more functional status by enabling the brain to self-regulate itself. This means it can heal psychological wounds as well as combat addiction. Additionally, because the technique is non-verbal and targets brain behaviour directly, it bypasses the type of resistance therapists can encounter.

Othmer feels that family members should do Neurofeedback as well as the drinkers as they should benefit, too, but without doing as much. The approach leads to better brain function for anyone, particularly stressed-out people, so it has definite application to care-givers, relatives and associates of the implicated individual.

'When such individuals are involved it will make the process of recovery more of a common journey for all involved,' says Othmer, 'and dissipate the stigma that tends to surround anything labelled therapy which targets mental function.'

For further information on Neurofeedback, visit www.eeginfo.com

In summary

- There can obviously be risks in using little-researched methods, but if someone is going to die without effective treatment these risks could be worth taking

- Only use these new methods in conjunction with medical advice and keep your eyes and ears open for relevant new research updates. Also be alert to the possibility of other exciting new developments becoming available

- Don't be put off by negative opinions from conventional practitioners who haven't yet paid serious attention to the newer methods, and if a doctor is not familiar with the Sinclair Method, take them a copy of the letter on page 164 and, if they are not familiar with the Ameisen Baclofen Programme, take them a copy of The End of My Addiction

CHAPTER SEVEN

Looking After Yourself

You are not responsible for someone else's dependency on alcohol and should not feel guilty about it, although we appreciate that this can be a hard message to take on board if you love someone.

You are, on the other hand, very much responsible for your own wellbeing and, if you have been close to a heavy drinker, your mental and even physical health will almost certainly have been adversely affected. Instigating your own recovery will not necessarily be easy, but the basic principles involved are extremely straightforward. You also require outside help. This explains why, although this is one of our most important chapters, it is also one of the shortest.

Partners and family members of problem drinkers, in particular, are likely to have become anxious, angry, full of fear and ashamed. Ironically these are the same feelings that the drinker themselves will be experiencing and, like the drinker, you may also be in denial about your problem. Even if you are not, then you will be desperate to talk to someone about it. But the stigma attached to alcoholism and the belief that it 'should never have happened to a family like yours' will probably prevent you from seeking the help you need.

This pent-up emotion and frustration will have started to affect your life in many ways and, without help, your symptoms will only get worse. Your own closest relationships and job will suffer and you will take out your hurt and fear on those who love you most. This will probably not include the drinker for fear that being too honest about how you are affected will drive them deeper into their addiction. This tiptoeing around the drinker often goes on for years.

You are likely to be decidedly lacking in self-esteem. Just like the drinker, you may well over-react to comments and gestures from others that were not intended to be threatening and your life will probably revolve almost entirely around alcohol. You may well have started losing touch with reality because the coping mechanisms you have developed involve denying that anything unusual or unpleasant is happening.

'In order to accommodate and survive the progression of the alcoholic's disease or a loved one's excessive drinking (alcohol abuse), the people who love him (or her) have had to adapt and change their thinking and behaviours and join in the denial protecting it. In other words, they've had to adopt their own version of denial.'

Lisa Frederiksen from *If You Loved Me, You'd Stop!*

What is Co-dependency?

Definitions of co-dependency vary markedly, and at one extreme they can apply to virtually everyone who has any form of relationship with another human being. In its simplest sense the term refers to someone who is unhealthily dependent on someone else's behaviour.

Just as we do not feel that whether or not you regard alcoholism as a disease is a major issue, we don't feel that whether you regard co-dependency as a disease is terribly important either. What matters is what you do to overcome it. It is also important that you should not regard yourself as in any way inferior just because you have developed symptoms of co-dependency. The chances are that you developed these behavioural patterns simply to protect yourself. You can therefore view yourself as having been largely a victim of circumstance, but circumstances to which you contribute and of which you are now an integral part.

In addition to saving you a huge amount of time, by learning to take greater care of your own needs rather than endlessly focusing on those of the drinker in your life, you can improve the healthy relationships in your life, such as those with family, people in the workplace and other areas of your personal life.

Co-dependents who don't address their problems often end up marrying other people with drink problems or, indeed, developing drink problems themselves.

Remember also another recurring theme of this book. You will not just be helping yourself by focusing on your own recovery. You will also be helping the drinker because, by pandering to their needs, you will have been propping up their condition.

Beverley Owen, Family Group Facilitator for ADAS, an alcohol and drug charity based in Stockport in Cheshire, says, 'Co-dependency becomes a problem when one person is relying on the behaviour of someone else. For example, if the drinker comes home very miserable and depressed, then the co-dependent relies on their behaviour because it makes them feel better trying to help. This can be a problem when the drinker comes back from recovery a different person, because the co-dependent person doesn't get the same rewards. In some ways they may subconsciously be wishing them to get ill again so they can continue the unhealthy relationship. This is very common.'

'Families have rules which need to be verbalized, and to be fair and flexible. Rules such as "no hitting", or "everyone will have a chance to be heard", lead to healthier functioning within a system. In alcoholic family structures, should rules be established, they are usually not based on a need for healthy protection, but instead are built on shame, guilt or fear.'

Claudia Black from *It Will Never Happen To Me!*

■ **CASE STUDY** A Bird's Eye View of Co-dependency

Fifty-four-year-old HR consultant Becky Stuart did not become co-dependent with her father to anything like the extent her mother did, but she points out that her father's life was inseparably interlinked with hers while she lived at home during her school days.

'I couldn't bring anyone back to the house,' she recalls. 'Originally when I was thirteen or fourteen I did bring very close friends back, but I tried to avoid doing so. He was drunk and abusive and, because we had no money as a result of his drinking, the sofas and carpets had holes in them and everything needed decorating. The fact that we lived in a council house also had a certain stigma because we had lost our nice home when I was ten. I will never forget the times when I heard the bailiffs coming round and my mother told me not to answer the door.'

'When I was older the situation didn't help my marriage, either. My husband refused to visit my parents so I always had to go and see them on my own. On my wedding day I had to beg my dad to be on his best behaviour and threatened not to talk to him again if he caused a scene. Fortunately he didn't. The irony was that my husband's parents didn't drink.'

'Mum had no opinion on anything and felt worthless. She would always stick up for him because she absolutely adored him.'

In some respects Becky, who is now divorced and lives in Southampton, assumed the role of father, helping out around the home, babysitting and looking after her two younger brothers and younger sister when they came home from school. Her father, who died of cirrhosis of the liver in 1988, was unable to work for the last five years of his life, so her mother had to go out to work.

'She became a doormat,' explains Becky. 'She cooked all the meals and did all the housework while all he did was drink. By the time he died he was drinking two or three bottles of vodka a day. Mum had no opinion on anything and felt worthless. She would always stick up for him because she absolutely adored him. He would come home from the pub and yell at us both, but the next morning he would wake up whistling and cheerful, and if I ever mentioned the night before, Mum would tell me not to speak about my father like that.

'On one occasion, when she was out, he threw me across the room, but she refused to believe me and told me my father would never do anything like that. She wouldn't discuss his drinking with anyone except with one friend, who died of cancer a few years after Dad died. I'm still very frustrated that my mother allowed herself to be so co-dependent over the years. She's had a very sad life and it's a real shame she didn't go to Al-Anon, but however hard I tried to persuade her to do so she just wouldn't do it. Even after he died she said that it would be too embarrassing to go and that you shouldn't hang out your dirty linen in public.'

> 'I am still very frustrated that my mother allowed herself to be so co-dependent over the years. She's had a very sad life and it's a real shame she didn't go to Al-Anon.'

Her mother refused to go for any kind of counselling either, but Becky did what she could to help her recover from her co-dependency. At one point she even went to live with her for a few months, but this proved a mistake because she found that her mother started to depend on her just as she had depended on her late husband.

'Mum now talks to me more openly about the past and I think this has helped,' explains Becky. 'I think I have helped her gain confidence and she has started doing more things for herself. She has bought a place and done it up, but she still struggles with relationships and continues to be private and self-sacrificing. She is always surprised if neighbours invite her round or anyone shows any interest in getting to know her. But at least she now goes out shopping and goes to an evening class once a week.

'When I was in my twenties I was determined not to become co-dependent like my mother. In particular, I decided never to have children as I didn't want to feel trapped and I didn't want anyone to be dependent on me.'

Overcoming Co-dependency

As with overcoming a drink problem, the first stage in overcoming co-dependency is recognizing that you have a problem in the first place. It is all too easy to take the 'ostrich approach' and bury your head in the sand in the hope that everything will go away. It won't. As with drink problems, delay equals deterioration.

'Denial is your biggest enemy. It seems impossible to believe that you are involved with an alcoholic. It simply cannot be true. If it cannot be true, it isn't true. You believe what you want to believe. You ignore reality.'

Janet Geringer Woititz from *Marriage on the Rocks*

You may feel anxious or guilty when the drinker has a problem and feel compelled to help them solve it, or you may suffer from low self-esteem and depression, suppress feelings, worry unduly about the silliest of things, check on the drinker far too often and desperately seek approval from others. These are merely some of the many symptoms of co-dependency, and each individual will be affected differently and by a different combination of traits. The key danger signal to watch out for is simply whether you are paying more attention to the drinker's wellbeing than to your own.

Experts stress that an important starting point in combating denial and beginning to feel better is starting to talk about your situation to other people. That doesn't mean broadcasting everything to the entire neighbourhood, but identifying at least one person who is likely to understand or be sympathetic. As we have already explained, feeling ashamed of the condition and not being able to accept that this could happen to a family like yours is one of the biggest obstacles to feeling well.

You cannot address this all on your own. Even if you have someone to confide in, they may never have experienced the horror and reality of addiction themselves. By attending Al-Anon (see pages 189 to 194) or other local self-help groups you will get to know many people with exactly the same first-hand experience.

Attendance will also help you greatly with the core task of detachment, which essentially is the process of learning how to lead your own life and developing your own thought patterns without them centring around someone else's drinking the whole time. You should also start to apply this attitude of detachment to others in your life, not just the drinker.

'Learning to detach from other people with love allows us to place a healthy emotional distance between ourselves and our loved ones without abandoning them. In the simplest terms, we find out where we leave off and others begin.'

From Survival to Recovery (Al-Anon Family Groups)

Experts emphasize the importance of those who have become co-dependent finding more 'me time', and many advise them to make a list of the things they like doing and to make a point of doing one of them every day. These can range from reading a book or phoning a friend for a chat to having a massage or facial. Taking up new hobbies and pastimes, especially those that make you feel relaxed and comfortable, are commonly recommended, as are attending courses on subjects of interest.

In short, anything that can help switch the emphasis away from the drinker and onto yourself is likely to be positive. At the same time, try not to fight back or react to the drinker's unpleasant behaviour. This task is likely to become even more challenging as the drinker starts to resent the changes you are making to your life, but the key is simply to realize that they are not well.

When under the influence, their wish to consume alcohol supersedes all other needs and desires, and they are no longer the person you have known or loved. To ask someone with a serious physical addiction why they can't just stop and control their drinking is pointless as even the addict doesn't know the answer. All they know is that when they get a craving for alcohol then alcohol will make them feel better.

We have spoken to many family members who have forgotten about even the simplest of pleasures as all their time and energy is consumed by thinking about the drinker and fearing for the future. Someone said to us recently, 'All I want in my life is peace, but I can't have that because of the problems addiction has brought on me and my family.' It is up to you whether you allow alcohol addiction to destroy you and your family. You deserve to hear the birds sing and walk in the country without fear and trepidation.

A pretty good starting point is to become familiar with Al-Anon's serenity prayer and to refer to it when you feel in need of help or need to remind yourself that there are some things over which you are powerless.

THE SERENITY PRAYER

God grant me the serenity
To accept the things I cannot change,
Courage to change the things I can,
And wisdom to know the difference.

For those wanting detailed practical guidance on the art of detachment, we would recommend reading some of the books detailed in our further reading section (see pages 225 to 226). We would also strongly advise enlisting the services of a suitable counsellor to help you with detachment. You have probably never spent enough time on 'you' or had the courage or knowledge to establish boundaries that will help you live a fulfilled and independent life. Help from such third parties can also be invaluable in assisting with the task of trying to correct some of the personality traits you may have developed as a result of adapting to having a problem drinker in your life.

'You'll know that you've found detachment when you can feel empathy for the alcoholic's drinking and behaviour, when you can accept constructive criticism without the old feeling of failure, and when you can hear impassioned but dishonest pleas without giving into them. You'll know you've found detachment when you're accused falsely and don't feel guilty, when you can laugh at the funny things in your life, when you can cry and not care who sees it, when you can show anger in a positive way.'

Evelyn Leite from *Detachment*

Counsellors can be particularly helpful when it comes to addressing low self-worth and helping people start to value themselves more as human beings.

Madeleine Moore at Workscales says of co-dependents, 'They are often carrying little voices around in their heads saying that they're no good, so they should consider asking friends and family what's good about them. They will probably feel embarrassed about it, but they might be pleasantly surprised by the results.'

She recalls one particular client who said that people didn't value her opinions. When she asked this individual's opinion of a glass ashtray on the table she initially offered none, but when the client was really made to think she realized she could in fact offer opinions and this really pleased her.

Moore advises that those with low self-worth should start watching programmes like *Question Time* and try to form opinions on issues of the day and as many other things as possible. Instead of letting people always giving them *their* opinions, they could start asserting their own views and discussing what they need from a relationship, as opposed to simply being told what their role is. She emphasizes that it can be a bumpy path to start with, but that it can bring people closer together eventually.

Moore also recommends confidence building and assertiveness training with counsellors and trainers to help build self-esteem, and suggests books on assertiveness. Couples counselling is also highlighted as a good source of help, as long as it is with a professionally trained counsellor, such as those employed by the Marriage Guidance Council. Whilst acknowledging that it can be hard to get the drinker to attend, she points out that the drinker's partner could start off by going on their own, then stress how important the relationship is and invite their other half to join in.

'The partner who doesn't have a drink problem often colludes with the partner who does have one and ends up drinking nearly as much, otherwise they become the enemy,' Moore continues. 'So once again it's about being assertive. They could inform the drinker that they are worried about their health and say that if they want to drink then it's up to them.'

Group sessions for family members can also shed valuable light on the different roles that each member of the family has with a problem drinker. One, for example, may be the 'chronic enabler', another 'the hero' and another 'the joker'. All are causing damage and all may have to make serious adjustments to the way they interact with the drinker once they have gone dry.

ADAS's Beverley Owen says, 'The joker may feel helpless as it doesn't seem appropriate to make people laugh any more, and the hero might not feel needed as there is no one to save any more. We would encourage as many family members as possible to come one evening a week for family groups, but if they can manage to come more often, so much the better. We normally get parents, partners or siblings, although we rarely get more than two people from each family.

'It can be helpful for them to work out their role in the family and, because these people are vulnerable, we take a very quiet approach and avoid counselling speak. Children of alcoholics are also very much part of the family role scenario. They are too young to be adults and therefore end up being carers so, unless they receive treatment, later in life they subconsciously look for partners who need to be cared for and often end up marrying addicts.'

'Recovery is not only fun, it is simple. It is not always easy, but it is simple. It is based on a premise many of us have forgotten or never learned. Each person is responsible for him- or herself. It involves learning one new behaviour that we will devote ourselves to: taking care of ourselves.'

Melody Beattie from *Codependent No More*

As when trying to find methods to help the drinker, it's important to keep your eyes and ears open in the search for the form of counselling that's most likely to be effective for you. Comparing notes with others in similar situations, whom you can identify with, and listening to personal recommendations is important, as is keeping an open mind to new developments. For example, at the time of writing, a new form of counselling called the 5-Step Method is beginning to receive quite a few plaudits.

The 5-Step Method focuses on the type of experiences that family members of the addicts face on a daily basis and the exploration of their circumstances, but does not see the family member as a cause or significant contributor to the development of the addiction problem. It sees them just as ordinary people facing a very challenging problem and feels they have the capacity to cope and respond to an addiction problem, just as people are able to cope with a range of very difficult and complex problems in life. (For further information on this, see www.alcoholdrugsandfamilies.nhs.uk.)

■ CASE STUDY A Combination of Al-Anon and Therapist Helps Overcome Co-dependency

As the oldest child, Thomas felt he had no one to call out to when his parents fought, so invariably he just froze in bed and listened . . . to continuous verbal, physical and even sexual violence. On one occasion his father even brought home another man for a threesome.

By the age of sixteen he had graduated to intervening and having fist fights with his dad, who remained a high-functioning salesman. Drinking seemed to have little impact on his ability to make money and he would plan all his business appointments accordingly: all non-drinking meetings took place earlier in the day and boozier individuals were granted pride of place later in the evening.

Thomas, who is now a fifty-four-year-old teacher, explains, 'When I was young it seemed like my mum was sick and Dad just came home and went to bed. I often took my father's side, but as time went on I came to understand the damage that alcohol can cause to people. Nevertheless, I had no idea what was wrong with my mother, who used me as a counsellor and confidante. This caused me a lot of psychological damage and one of my biggest challenges later in life was to get rid of my co-dependency with her.

'It was only really between the ages of thirty and thirty-four that it hit me how much the problem had affected me in later life. I realized that I had a substantial need to be with people who needed me and that I got a great deal of comfort from being in situations when I was able to fix people, whether it was my mother, partners or students. I was an approval seeker, looking for approval in any way I could. I also started having problems with my physical image, even though I feel I've always been a pretty good-looking guy. I would refuse to have my photo taken and hated buying new clothes as I couldn't face looking in the mirror.'

'I realized that I had a substantial need to be with people who needed me and that I got a great deal of comfort from being in situations when I was able to fix people.'

'I thought it was about love, but it was about fear,' he continues. 'The fear of someone getting close, and also the conflicting fear of being alone. What started out as being wonderful, in each case turned into craziness, and I was incapable of being honest with anyone, even though that was what I yearned for. It was like being a hamster on a wheel: endless activity but at the end of the day I was still in exactly the same spot as I when I'd started.'

Thomas, whose parents divorced when he was twenty-seven, but who are both still alive, bottled everything up during his schooldays, and did well both academically and at music. The fact that he started going to Alateen meetings once a week from the age of twelve onwards at least gave him a group of peers with whom to discuss his father's drinking, but otherwise he never mentioned the subject to anyone except his mother – not even his younger sister.

Switching from Alateen to Al-Anon at the age of twenty, he has attended regularly for most of his adult life, barring a three-year break between the ages of thirty and thirty-three. However, whilst his attendance up until this break proved highly beneficial, it could not help him avoid making the 'text book' mistake of getting involved with as many as three women who turned out to have drink problems. One of these relationships lasted eight years and the couple were married for three of them.

'They all hid it pretty well,' recalls Thomas, who is now happily co-habiting in a ten-year strong relationship. 'The fact that they all knew about my father right from the word go probably made them extra careful to conceal things. I didn't even realize my wife had a drink problem until after we'd got married, which seems incredible in the light of my experience with my father and considering that my grandmother and several members of my less immediate family died of drink problems.'

> 'Apart from anything else, Al-Anon is great
> fun. There's a terrific amount of humour and
> I would say that most of my best
> friends are from there.'

A combination of returning to Al-Anon once a week from his early thirties onwards, and six years of regular counselling with a therapist, have proved highly liberating, and Thomas, who admits that he only really started understanding his mother when he began to understand himself, says he is a 'very happy man'.

'The counselling was particularly successful as I had a therapist who didn't talk much and we did a lot of acting things out. I had major anger issues and he would provoke rage attacks, which helped me realize that underlying my anger was terror, and that I was afraid of everybody and everything. I used my anger as a protection mechanism to hide my fear.

'Al-Anon and the therapist have helped me brilliantly. Al-Anon taught me that I was not doing any good for those in my life by taking over all responsibility for their actions.

Being powerless is quite freeing as it means that I am not responsible. I am not religious and I can assure anyone who has reservations that you don't have to be religious to benefit from Al-Anon.

'Even though I am now way better, I expect I'll always go to Al-Anon because I believe it's a process of never-ending self-discovery and that without its support I might revert back. Apart from anything else, Al-Anon is great fun. There's a terrific amount of humour and I would say that most of my best friends are from there.'

Al-Anon

Whatever type of counselling you have and however much material you read, attending a local self-help group regularly is likely to prove the single most important factor in learning the art of detachment and in overcoming the problem of co-dependency. Wherever you live in the world, Al-Anon, which has over 25,000 groups worldwide, is likely to be the most available option. Meetings for Al-Anon and Alateen – the equivalent group for those aged under 20 (see Chapter 8, pages 199 to 203) – are now held in 134 countries.

For the Al-Anon General Service Office in London, which provides English meeting information for all of Europe, Asia and Africa (with the exception of South Africa) as well as the UK, visit http://www.al-anon.alateen.org/meetings/unitedkingdom.html. For the US and Canada, and countries which do not have a national office of their own, visit www.al-anon.alateen.org.

Al-Anon offers relatives and friends of those with drink problems the chance to share their experiences, strengths and hopes in order to solve their common problems and to put the focus back on their own lives in a healthy and loving way. It believes that alcoholism is a family illness – as opposed to something that just affects the drinker – and that changing attitudes can assist in recovery.

Anyone whose life is, or has been, affected by someone else's drinking is able to participate in closed meetings. Open meetings, which are less common, can be attended by anyone interested in or learning about the family disease of alcoholism. Meetings, which typically last for between one and two hours, are opened with a moment of silence and closed with a prayer. They are led by a member serving as a chairperson for that weekly meeting, who asks others to talk about how Al-Anon has helped them. There is no compulsion for anyone attending to speak themselves, though. If they prefer, they can just listen.

> 'I was afraid to lose the only people who said they loved me. I was afraid they wouldn't come back, and then I was afraid they would. It was confusing. People said they loved me and then they hurt me. In my gut, I knew something was wrong, but I was told I over-reacted or that I was too sen-sitive, so I learned not to trust my instincts.'
>
> *From Survival To Recovery* (Al-Anon Family Groups)

The basic Al-Anon philosophy is that only those who have actually lived with someone with a serious drink problem and who've experienced the very real pain that goes with the ordeal can understand the problems of other people in similar situations, and that once they realize they are powerless over alcohol they are free of a huge burden.

There are obvious similarities to AA in that, although Al-Anon is not for drinkers themselves, attendance is free – although groups commonly have a collection to cover expenses – only first names are used to ensure anonymity, and both new and existing members can secure the help of a sponsor to aid them in the recovery process.

A sponsor, as well as sharing their own experiences and providing personal support, can explain the Al-Anon programme and, should the member choose to do so, help work and apply the 12 Steps. Like those of AA – which they are similar but not identical to – the 12 Steps make frequent references to God but, once again, Al-Anon is a spiritual as opposed to a religious organization and requires only a belief in a higher power, which can even be the group itself.

Unlike AA, towards which opinion tends to be somewhat divided, it is most unusual to hear anything other than unmitigated praise for Al-Anon, from either alcohol experts or from those who attend the meetings. When reservations are expressed it tends to be from those who attended a single meeting and clearly chose a group that was not best suited to them. As with AA, groups can vary in terms of format and atmosphere, and it is advisable to try a number of different ones initially.

Many members eventually identify a meeting they feel they want to attend on a regular basis, which is known as their 'home group'. Having a home group can provide obvious advantages as it makes it easier to strike up close relationships with other members and can also make it easier to find a sponsor.

If there is no Al-Anon group in your area, there is nothing stopping any two or three relatives of those with drink problems from starting up their own group, as long as they have no other affiliation outside Al-Anon. Alternatively, those without access to a local group, or who are housebound, can benefit from a Lone Member Service, which enables them to write letters to members who regularly attend face-to-face meetings.

Online Al-Anon provides a further option, giving members access to groups that exchange emails, real-time meetings with other members via chat rooms and to Internet telephony meetings, which allow members who install special software and equipment to meet real-time via free conference calls over the Internet so they can hear the voices of other members.

An alternative to Al-Anon is offered by Co-Dependents Anonymous (CoDA), which provides a 12-Step-based approach to those co-dependent with users of other drugs as well as alcohol. This already provides meetings in well over a dozen different languages (for UK see www.coda-uk.org, or for US, www.coda. org). Additionally, you may find that there are other independent groups who meet in your area for friends and families of those with drink problems. These are not always 12-Step based and some allow drinkers to attend alongside their loved ones.

■ CASE STUDY Learning From a Self-Help Group

Forty-seven-year-old nurse Alison Breaker admits that she has never been particularly close to her younger brother Tony, and the fact that he doesn't live with her means that she is playing a slightly different ball game to many others affected by a family member or partner's drinking. Nevertheless, this did not prevent her from developing at least a degree of co-dependent behaviour, and her message to anyone who finds themselves in a similar predicament is to join a self-help group.

'I would wake up in the night sick with worry,' she explains, 'but I have now toughened up a bit and the group has made me realize that he is on his own journey. Attending has given me so many ideas about how to behave towards him and how to talk to him. He would say that he'd heard people can't recover, but I can now demonstrate knowledge and say that they can in fact recover.

'The one thing that really opened my eyes was the constant discussion about the difference between tough love and enabling. I realized that I had been spending an awful lot of time sorting out his financial affairs, phoning people about help for him and generally rushing around on his behalf. They advised me to step back and to start getting used to the idea that he must do more to help himself.'

'I have now toughened up a bit and the group has made me realize that he is on his own journey.'

The family support group that Alison attends in her home town is different from Al-Anon in that it's not 12-Step orientated. Nevertheless, the meetings work in a way that is not dissimilar to Al-Anon, enabling friends and loved ones of drinkers to bare their souls in confidence and to benefit from the support and experience of those in similar situations. Most others who attend have partners or children with drink problems, but she is the only person she has noticed who's been suffering because of a sibling.

Tony, who is forty-four and doesn't have a partner, had started drinking particularly heavily five years ago after being made redundant from a job he really loved in the retail industry. Although he found a new job in the same industry, he didn't enjoy it much and, having become unemployed again within a year, he hasn't worked since. Although he still lives in his own house, he once nearly had it repossessed, but was helped out by Alison's husband Frank, who has since been repaid from the equity of Tony's house.

'On one occasion we were particularly upset when he went on a bender after we'd given him some money,' Alison recalls. 'So once he was feeling a bit less ill we told him we couldn't keep helping him financially if he continued to abuse alcohol. Our stance probably made him realize that we wouldn't be messed around with. I think the tough-love attitude helped, but in fairness to him he was probably heading in the right direction anyway.'

> 'They advised me to step back and to start getting used to the idea that he must do more to help himself.'

One advantage that Alison has over many family members and friends of those with drink problems is that Tony has never been in denial. He has always demonstrated an awareness that he needs to give up, even though he hasn't managed to do so for more than a few months. After undergoing two detoxes and finding there wasn't space for a third on the NHS, he decided to try and cut down in conjunction with help from local support groups.

During the last six months he has lost a lot of weight and, according to the drink diary he's been keeping, he seems to have managed to keep within the Government's safe-drinking guidelines. He brings the drink diary with him when he attends a monthly counselling session with Alison, but apart from this regular session, she doesn't really see much of him.

'He does look a lot better and I believe he's drinking at the levels he says, but I'm still not 100 per cent convinced because of the previous relapses that have occurred after he's said that everything is sorted. He is looking for employment and I think that if he gets a break he will make the most of it. I will give him all the emotional support he needs, but I won't give him any money. Even though he seems to be doing OK at the moment he can still be a bit illogical, and he's not quite as good at living within his means as he should be.'

In summary

- Always remember that you are not responsible for another person's drinking, but that you are responsible for your own wellbeing, and you may well have become unhealthily dependent on someone else's behaviour

- Start to focus on your own needs, and by helping yourself you will also be helping the drinker

- Start to talk about your situation with suitable individuals, enlist the help of an appropriate counsellor and attend self-help group meetings

- Familiarize yourself with some of the books in our further reading section, which aim to help with detachment and to correct co-dependency

CHAPTER EIGHT

Looking After Children of Problem Drinkers, Both Young and Adult

Every child who grows up in a home where one or both parents have a serious drink problem is going to be adversely affected, and if the problem is not addressed it is likely to have serious consequences for their future happiness. Indeed, it could also have an unhealthy impact on their children and even grandchildren.

People whose parents have a drink problem are far more likely to end up having drink problems themselves. Another common trait is that the children of drinkers are highly prone to end up marrying people with drink problems, even though they tend not to be aware of the fact at the time they get married.

As discussed for co-dependent family members in general in Chapter 7, the lives of children with a parent who drinks often become consumed by fear and guilt and they adopt coping strategies to survive that need to be corrected if they're going to move on and lead a happy and fulfilled life. Some experts emphasize that adult children of drinkers tend to have no experience of what is and isn't 'normal' and they find it hard to follow projects through from beginning to end.

'For children in the family, the combination of alcoholism and co-alcoholism results in neither parent being responsive and available on a consistent, predictable basis.

> Children are affected not only by the alcoholic parent, but also by the non-alcoholic parent (if there is one) and by the abnormal family dynamics created as a consequence of alcoholism.'
>
> Claudia Black from *"It Will Never Happen To Me!"*

The experience of having an alcoholic parent can affect children in different ways, even if they are members of the same family. Many find it makes it difficult for them to express feelings, because denying their own feelings has been a key survival mechanism. They have probably never shared their inner-most thoughts and feelings with even their closest friends. Because their relationship with the drinker involved constantly being told lies and being let down, they have got into the habit of not trusting others and not relying on anyone else for help. Even when they know they need help they tend to find it very hard to ask for it.

This doesn't necessarily mean it will be obvious they are in need of help or should be a cause for concern during their formative years. Indeed they often appear quite normal and can excel academically or on the sports fields. But, if they do not receive help while they are young, problems often become evident when they are in their twenties, thirties or even forties, when they may experience feelings of loneliness and depression.

In their book, *Recovery: A Guide for Adult Children of Alcoholics*, Herbert L. Gravitz and Julie D. Bowden, observe an interesting correlation. The US based co-authors, who are founding members of the board of directors of the National Association for Children of Alcoholics, point out that it seems to be true that the adverse impact of someone having lived in a family that contains someone with a serious drink problem tends to become greater both the younger the child is as the parent's drink problem progresses and the greater the length of time that the child actually ends up living with that problem drinker.

If the children of problem drinkers receive help whilst they are still young, it can greatly reduce the chances of them having to deal with the consequences of this belated time bomb. But, as the problem drinker is most unlikely to provide such help, the onus is on the partner without a drink problem – if there is one – to provide help and support.

Helping Them When They Are Still Young

If you are the non-drinking partner of a drinker and you have children, by changing your behaviour and examining your own issues you can make a huge difference to the way your children are impacted by your partner. By looking after yourself, dealing with any co-dependency issues and getting your life in order you can have a profoundly positive effect on your children.

Cat Payne, Practitioner and Tutor at Families Plus – part of the national charity Action on Addiction – which supports families, says, 'Research shows that the poor quality of family relationships is more damaging to children than the drinking itself. Children often feel they need to take responsibility for their drinking parent and, for example, hide the alcohol or throw it away.

'Children become hyper-vigilant and are always looking for "triggers". For example, if Dad's favourite football team loses a match, they might try to hide the alcohol or stop him going to the pub. They develop ways of coping and are always trying to make things "right" at home, even though circumstances are beyond their control. A child might make Dad or Mum their favourite supper, hoping to please them and make things better so that he or she won't drink that evening.'

In the event of domestic violence, children sometimes try to intervene between parents, which is dangerous and can result in the child getting hurt, both physically and emotionally. A child cannot stop two adults fighting, especially if one of them is drunk. The sober parent should, therefore, make sure that the child has the phone number, and permission to use it, of someone trustworthy who lives nearby and who will support the child should any violence occur.

Payne points out that it can also help if parents give the child permission to let them know if they don't have enough essential provisions as she sometimes sees children convicted of shoplifting who are too frightened to tell the court that they stole because they had no food or clean clothes.

'This is the result of a code of secrecy that can exist in alcoholic families,' she continues. 'A non-drinking parent who remains in a relationship with an alcoholic partner will often be involved in denial and covering up the problems, so they tell their children not to talk about it to anyone outside the family.'

Alateen

In an ideal world, the partner who doesn't have a drink problem should encourage their child to regularly attend Alateen, the sister organization of Al-Anon for those aged twelve to twenty with relatives or friends with serious drink problems. Each Alateen meeting is usually sponsored by two experienced Al-Anon members.

Contact details for Alateen are the same as for Al-Anon. For the Al-Anon General Service Office in London, providing English meeting information for all of Europe, Asia, and Africa (except South Africa) in addition to the UK, visit http://www.al-anon. alateen.org/meetings/unitedkingdom.html. For the USA, Canada and countries that do not have a national office of their own, visit www.al-anon.alateen.org.

'We lived in a small town and what was most difficult was the shame. There was no one to share the pain with. When a parent is an alcoholic there is no normal, just abnormal. I've had counselling but I certainly regret the fact that I didn't attend Alateen when I was younger. No one seemed to know about it in those days.'

Anonymous quote from a 45-year-old adult child of an alcoholic

Attending Alateen meetings can enable youngsters to gain an understanding of why the parent with a drink problem behaves in the way they do and to understand that it is not the child's fault. The realization that they are far from alone in having a parent with a drink problem is likely to be hugely beneficial, as is the ability to share experiences, support each other and collectively address their problems and find hope for the future.

One of the problems of Alateen is that it is not nearly so widely available as Al-Anon. There are, in fact, only around 2,000 Alateen groups worldwide, which is less than a tenth of the number of Al-Anon groups. There can also be a logistical problem, because unless the meeting is near a train station or bus stop the sober parent will need to drive them there each time, and this may not always be possible.

If there is no group in your area, it should be quite possible to create your own group by joining forces with parents who are able to provide adult sponsors from Al-Anon. But even then, parents often still find they have problems getting their children to attend Alateen meetings. Some children resist strongly, complaining that they would prefer to play football or indulge in other pastimes they enjoy. If so, the parent may well be forced to conclude that there is not a lot more they can do to ensure compliance at this particular point in time.

'I didn't know who I was before I came to Alateen. I acted like someone else so I could get people to be friends with me. As a result, I never really got to know what I was like. Now that I'm in Alateen , I've realized that it's OK to be who I am. If people don't like who I am, that's their problem. I also realized that it's good to cry sometimes. And it's real good to take time for myself.'

Anonymous Alateen member from *Courage to Be Me*

■ CASE STUDY Alateen Teaches What is Normal

By helping out regularly as a sponsor at meetings, twenty-eight-year-old Ann-Marie Martins can see Alateen helping younger people in the same way as it helped her. Having been introduced to the self-help group at the age of fourteen by her grandmother, she feels it's probably the best gift she ever gave her.

'I can see it working for young people, even though they didn't necessarily think there was anything wrong with them when they started, just like I didn't think there was anything wrong with me,' she explains. 'At first it can feel like going to the dentist to some people, but once they've had their teeth fixed they're grateful they've been. These groups are very important if someone is co-dependent because they teach you what part of your life is yours and what part is someone else's, and that these other people can do things on their own. It's a wonderful tool.'

'I just thought it was normal that if someone you loved was sad about something then so were you.'

Ann-Marie, who is currently settled with a long-term partner in Auckland, New Zealand, originally had no idea her childhood wasn't normal, despite being the only child of a single mother with a serious drink problem.

'My mum never had any real coping skills to teach me,' she recalls. 'We moved around a lot and I went to nine different schools. I didn't know who I was or what I liked because my mum took me virtually everywhere with her and we pretty much lived in each other's pockets. Because I grew up surrounded by adults, I was good at liaising with adults, but I found it hard to relate to people of my own age. My feelings and emotions were all based on what Mum was doing, and if she was sad then I got sad and if she was angry then I got angry. I just thought it was normal that if someone you loved was sad about something then so were you.'

Despite this extraordinarily close relationship, Ann-Marie was completely oblivious to the fact that her mother had any kind of drink problem. The matter only came to light when the youngster was thirteen and her mother was dating a man who was soon to become her husband, in a marriage that lasted four years. Her mother's new partner persuaded her to go to AA and she succeeded in kicking the drink, remaining sober to this day. But for her daughter this new-found sobriety proved a real problem.

'I thought the first twelve months of her sobriety were horrible as she became a very different person,' explains Ann-Marie, who now works as a vet's assistant. 'Now that she was sober she wanted to be more of a parent than a friend, and I didn't like that so much. We used to do all the same things together, like going to see bands, and all my friends were her drinking friends. But she wasn't with that set any more. Sobriety brings so many changes to a household.'

Attending Alateen once a week between the ages of fourteen and twenty proved crucial in breaking the co-dependency between mother and daughter. The relationship between the two is still very open and Ann-Marie talks to her mother regularly and likes to include her a lot in her life. Nevertheless, she now also enjoys leading her own life and doing her own things.

'These groups are very important if someone is co-dependent because they teach you what part of your life is yours and what part is someone else's.'

'Alateen has helped with all sorts of things,' continues Ann-Marie. 'I had some crazy things going on in my head and I was very grateful that I could actually talk about them, and most of the time other people would giggle because they had thought of the same things themselves. Alateen gave me the tools to find out who I was and to have an independent life.

'It taught me a lot about boundaries and about detachment. It was a gradual process. I've learned that I can identify when my behaviour becomes unacceptable. I won't be a doormat but I've also learned that I don't want other people to feel bad.'

Other Sources of Help to Consider

If there is no Alateen group that meets in your area and no obvious chance of starting one, or if you simply cannot get your child to attend a meeting, there may be other valuable sources of help in your country or area that don't have quite the same international brand. Ideally, a child of a problem drinker needs someone they can speak to and trust, but trust is one commodity that's likely to have been in particularly short supply in their household.

It may be possible to arrange for them to see a school nurse or counsellor but, if not, conducting an Internet search is likely to be the best way of establishing what exists in the way of other external sources of help accessible in your neighbourhood.

'Recovery is about discovering and becoming your own true self, the essence that is you behind the masks you have put on and the personas you have played while you were trying to please the world around you and keep would-be predators away. What you did – adopting rules and roles to keep yourself a safe distance from others – also created a distance within yourself, a gap between the real you and that unreal, defensive other.'

Claudia Black from *Changing Course*

In some countries, children of people with drink problems are able to phone a confidential national helpline. The confidentiality of this service is an extremely important feature as callers are often breaking their family's 'code of silence' for the first time and may feel they are putting themselves at risk by being disloyal to their parents.

In the UK, for example, a free helpline offered by the National Association of Children of Alcoholics (NACOA) – Tel: 0800 358 3456, website: www.nacoa.org.uk – focuses on the individual caller, encouraging them to look at their own practical wants and needs, rather than those of the family. Callers, who have often become closed to their own emotions and have distanced themselves from what is happening in their everyday lives, are able to tell their story to more than one volunteer helpline counsellor, and they are listened to without judgement.

By recounting their experiences, callers start to feel less overwhelmed and begin a process of looking at issues individually, tackling life a day at a time, sometimes an hour at a time, or simply between calls. Important messages that are communicated include the fact that the child is not alone, is not responsible for their parent's drinking and cannot control it.

Hilary Henriques, chief executive at NACOA, says, 'Callers often feel overwhelmed by their situations. They use drink, drugs or other behaviours, such as eating disorders and self-harm, as a means of surviving difficulties at home and subsequent problems at school and in other social situations. As with their parents, these seemingly destructive behaviours become the solution to the problem. Callers tell us they drink because they feel it numbs the pain and they want to forget what's happened or that they drink with their mum because it's the only good times they have.'

NACOA finds that some callers have no one to confide in, whereas others simply need help in order to rehearse what to say to their parents and how to ask for help. The helpline counsellors are often the only adults the callers feel able to ask for help from with regard to growing up in today's world. NACOA can help them make informed choices without feeling that they have to be an adult, and it can provide age-appropriate information so they can explore their options. The call is always about the caller, relevant to their individual situation, directed by the caller and at his or her own pace.

Regular callers are supported in ways that might ordinarily come from parents or carers. Helpline counsellors may, for example, establish what youngsters can change, what they can do for themselves and what is not within their power, and it often comes as a relief to know that they've been battling against impossible odds. No two calls are the same and some callers are concerned about younger siblings because the roles of child and parent have become blurred, adding to the caller's sense of responsibility for what is happening.

Many NACOA callers benefit massively simply from acknowledging that there is, or has been, a problem. Indeed, some calls are from adult children who just want to know what they can do to help the drinker and they are unaware that they themselves can be affected by someone else's problem.

Neither the callers, nor their parents, are criticized, instead they are provided with factual information and encouraged to find positive ways to express themselves and to cope with their difficulties. Staying in the present, concentrating on practical solutions and taking account of the caller's choices leads to what might seem small triumphs in both planning, thinking things through and informed choice making. This may be the first time a caller has experienced positive outcomes for themselves and it's a powerful lesson – one which may lead to future positive choices.

'Our work is about planning for a more positive future,' continues NACOA's Hilary Henriques. 'Positive experiences lead to higher self-esteem, a sense of autonomy and independence and the ability to perceive experiences constructively. It is common for children of alcohol-dependent parents to feel they are the problem, that they are to blame for it and that they are the cause of the problem.'

NACOA research has in fact found that children of alcohol-dependent parents are likely to feel almost six times more responsible for conflict in the home than children of non-alcohol-dependent parents. They are also seven times more likely to try and resolve arguments within the family. Research also shows that secrecy, manipulation and an inability to identify one's feelings are twice as likely to be prevalent within an alcohol-dependent family than within a family not affected by alcoholism, and that irrational behaviour is five times more likely to be prevalent.

Henriques says, 'Life is very confusing in an environment where alcohol affects the behaviour of one of the parents. It is difficult to predict the mood of the parent with the drink problem and the whole family begins to tell lies to cover up for the family member's drinking. Many children therefore feel too embarrassed to take friends home.

Local self-help groups may be available specifically to help the children of problem drinkers, and they may not necessarily be 12-Step based. In some cases these may involve the attendance of other family members as well.

■ CASE STUDY Family Programme Boosts Self-Confidence

It was Tim Bostock's decision to stop seeing his father in February 2009, even though he had being paying him regular visits in the aftermath of his parents' divorce eight years earlier. Tim, who is now fourteen years old, had simply had enough of hearing denial, especially when it came to how drinking hadn't played any part in the breakdown of his marriage.

His dad wouldn't drink every night and continued to be a high-functioning and plausible individual in the workplace. Nevertheless, his frequent binges resulted in him becoming 'absolutely vile' and he was often physically violent and had affairs with other women while he was married.

Up until the age of five, when his parents finally ended their seven-year marriage, Tim had become used to seeing them constantly rowing in front of him and witnessing his mother Wendy being shouted at and sometimes physically pushed against the sitting-room wall.

> 'Wendy was acutely aware of the fact that her son needed professional help if he was going to be able to lead anything approaching a normal life in the future.'

Even after the divorce, his father's drinking continued to have a deeply disturbing effect on the youngster. At the tender age of seven Tim found himself having to act like a responsible adult after the real adult – his dad – got so drunk that he collapsed in a caravan park. Somehow he had to try and get his dad back to the caravan! When Tim later arrived home he was too scared to tell his mother about the incident as he knew it would lead to arguments. She found out in due course, though, and stopped father and son from meeting for fifteen months.

'Eventually I allowed them to resume seeing each other because they clearly both wanted to do so,' explains forty-nine-year-old Wendy Bostock, who works as a librarian. 'It was easier not having Tim complaining all the time and, to be honest, I wasn't really sure whether he should be seeing his father or not. I am relieved that he was eventually able to make up his own mind not to see his father, although to begin with he was clearly still confused about the whole thing.

'I now have very little contact with his father, although I have never completely lost hope of him overcoming his drink problem. He is in a new relationship, but still texts me at about 2 a.m. when he is drunk once every couple of months.'

Nevertheless, Wendy was acutely aware of the fact that her son needed professional help if he was going to be able to lead anything approaching a normal life in the future. Finding herself unable to find a suitable local Alateen group in her home town of Bath, she eventually came across a programme called M-PACT (Moving Parents and Children Together), which was within driving distance. She decided that both Tim and she should attend this in July 2009.

> 'It reassured him that it was OK for him not to see his father and also reassured me on the subject.'

The ten-week M-PACT programme, run by national charity Action on Addiction, was designed to ensure that children and young people who know they have been overlooked realize that they have not been forgotten. By attending they realize that there are other people who recognize what they have to cope with in their daily lives, and they see that they can ask for help – if necessary from outside the family.

'The programme relaunched Tim,' enthuses Wendy. 'You work with your child, then split up into two groups of children and parents and then come back as a large group. It reassured him that it was OK for him not to see his father and also reassured me on the subject. He is far less confused about the issue now and realizes that he has valid reasons for not seeing his dad. As a family, it made us far more accepting of his father's condition and made us realize that we didn't want to see him.

'Tim has changed so much just by having a source of external help, and M-PACT has had a knock-on effect in other areas of his life, too, making him much more confident about his own judgement. He has even been confident enough to make a TV appearance helping the children of problem drinkers. I like to think he will now grow up to have a reasonably normal life and, because he has seen the impact of alcohol on our family, it will hopefully ensure he is careful with drink himself.

'The fact that he met children in the same position as himself on the course did him a lot of good as it enabled him to talk about things,' continues Wendy. 'Your father's drink problem isn't the type of thing you can talk about at school. He's still friendly with one of the children and contacts some of the others on Facebook. Unlike me, most of the other parents attending were alcoholics and drug addicts in recovery. Through this, Tim could see they were nice people who had gone off track for a while, and this made him realize that the major problem with his dad was the drink.'

Steps to Take When Children Are Older

Sources of help are not as plentiful as they should be for those who don't successfully resolve their issues during their childhood and consequently experience problems later in life. These are commonly referred to as Adult Children of Alcoholics (abbreviated here simply to 'adult children') and although, as discussed in Chapter 2, we are not overly keen on using the word 'alcoholic', we are happy to do so in this case because the description of this group is now so universally accepted that it has effectively become an official title.

Attending Al-Anon is widely recommended by many experts, and in many countries a further more specifically tailored 12-Step-based self-help group option is provided by Adult Children of Alcoholics meetings (www.adultchildren.org). Confidential national helplines such as the one offered by NACOA can also be used by adult children, as well as by their younger counterparts, and there are sources of further reading detailed in our Appendix 2, which are highly recommended. In addition to explaining the issues involved with being an adult child, these contain some valuable practical exercises that can be carried out in your own home.

Nevertheless, even if you use a combination of all these resources, we strongly recommend that you also enlist the services of an appropriate counsellor or therapist to help you develop the proactive coping skills required for getting over your problems and moving on.

'With grown-up children of alcoholics we notice a really profound sense of loss,' continues Cat Payne from Families Plus. 'They know they can never regain a relationship with their parents which they never had, so finding someone who understands, can listen and offer support is a help.'

Payne points out that there isn't as much support available for family members impacted by someone else's substance misuse as there is for families coping with conditions such as cancer, despite the stress being equally severe, if not more so, because of the culture of secrecy and shame that comes from living with addiction.

'We say to our clients you can't control addiction – it is like trying to control the weather,' she adds. 'If it's going to rain it's going to rain and you can't stop that, but we can support you and help you remember to take your umbrella and wellington boots.'

'Developing the skills necessary to establish positive emotional intimacy is the most critical developmental task for children of alcoholics. Intimacy problems begin when people push you away and reject you. The core of all intimacy problems is a fear that other people will abandon you.'

Robert. J. Ackerman from *Perfect Daughters*

John Friel is a licenced psychologist based in Minneapolis in the US and founder of the 3.5-day ClearLife Clinic, designed for people to uncover the family-of-origin roots of painful adult behaviour (see www.clearlife.com). He emphasizes that, although there are no universal rules, there are some spikes between the ages of nineteen to twenty-one, twenty-nine to thirty-one and thirty-nine to forty-three when adult children start to feel the pain of what's been going on. He stresses that, even if they are attending a self-help group, they still need a good therapist to 'install the missing part of the software they should have had installed as kids.'

Friel explains, 'We are all adult children from dysfunctional families because something happened to us a long time ago, and it happened more than once. We protected ourselves the best way we knew how and we are still protecting ourselves, but it isn't working any more. So unless we install that software we'll keep on making the same mistakes. We all subconsciously re-enact childhood patterns, and there are certain basic ways of dealing with feelings and relationships that get short-circuited, so it's really about growing up. You need to establish what strengths and limitations you grew up with, but not make the mistake of focusing too much on the negatives rather than the positives.'

He maintains that there is no such thing as a typical alcoholic family. Some are extremely hurtful whilst others are only moderately hurtful, so you can't say that everyone is damaged in the same way, and identifying what happened is a gradual unfolding process when people mature.

'We all try and hide things, but as long as you keep thinking it's not your problem and that it's someone else's problem you won't change,' he continues. 'We all act out ways of coping, but when people get to adulthood and start tripping over the ghosts of their pasts they often need to seek help. Take a look at yourself and ask whether you are the cause of what's going on in your life or is it everyone else's fault?'

Friel stresses that once you are an adult you can't keep blaming your childhood and using it as an excuse. Rather, you must identify where the problems came from. There is a difference between discovering the system and its rules so that you can grow up, and blaming. You need to ask what you can change and what part of yourself you have to look at and confront. Above all, you know you are becoming a healthy adult when you can choose the discomfort of loneliness rather than hurt yourself, hurt others or let others hurt you.'

CASE STUDY Attracted to a Younger Version of Her Father

A chance meeting in a shopping centre at the age of seven was to have major implications for Aimee Whitfield's future. She instantly recognized her father, whom she had not seen for four years, and he immediately recognized her.

'Mum had kicked him out and I think it was because of his drinking,' explains Aimee, who is now twenty-eight and has a four-month-old daughter. 'He used to break into our fifty-pence gas meter to get money for the pub, and when I was three he even once left me in the pub. The barmaid, who knew my mother, had to phone her to ask her to collect me.'

On hearing of the unplanned reunion and of the news that her former husband had now apparently quit drinking, Aimee's mother was prepared to let the two meet regularly. But at the age of eleven, Aimee received definitive proof that his sobriety had only been temporary. After inviting her and a friend round to his place for the day, her father disappeared almost as soon as he'd let them in. Staggering back drunk in the early evening, he tried unsuccessfully to get the girls to pay for his taxi fare and left them to do the cooking while he crashed out on his bed upstairs.

> 'Now that I'm a mother I don't want my daughter to go through what I went through.'

In spite of this, knowing that he had a new live-in partner to take care of him, Aimee's mother was prepared to allow Aimee to continue visiting her dad. Whenever Aimee was in his home and saw him fall asleep after knocking back the vodka, she would pour the remainder of the bottle down the sink. It made no difference, though, as he simply went out and bought more. Then, when Aimee was fifteen, he suddenly upped sticks and left his partner, landing her with a £400 bill for alcohol which he'd built up on a tab at a local shop.

After approaching the former partner for her dad's address a year later, Aimee traced her father to a flat in Portsmouth and, on visiting, found 'a mess' in a wheelchair, who was suffering from diabetes and incontinence. Even though he was still in denial about his drinking, Aimee continued to want to sort him out and help him. She bought him a video recorder and regularly tidied up and cooked for him, despite the fact that he was visited three times a day by state-funded carers. She still visits him in a care home where, at the age of only sixty-four, his memory has become almost non-existent.

Although she didn't realize it at the time, this unusual relationship with her father took a huge toll on Aimee's personal life. At the age of fifteen she was attracted to a twenty-five-year-old man who was almost the spitting image of her father. He had the same Irish descent as her father, the same physical appearance and the same personality. Like her father, he was very caring when sober, but very vicious when drunk. This unsatisfactory relationship lasted for ten years, on and off, before her partner left her in June 2007.

'I wish I'd had counselling or attended a self-help group at a much younger age. If I had done I think it would have prevented me getting involved with someone so like my father.'

'I was definitely Daddy's girl when he was sober,' explains Aimee, who has never drunk much herself. 'But because I never really had him around, I was drawn to someone who was almost identical. I had some counselling during the relationship and the counsellor said my partner and I were co-dependent. She was right, because when he left me I didn't know how to cope. I broke down and had panic attacks because I'd gone from having someone depend on me 24/7 and always phoning me to having total freedom, and I missed someone needing me.

'When he left me, I resolved not to have people in my life making decisions for me any longer,' Aimee continues. 'The therapist certainly helped as I had all these messages jumbled up in my head and she helped me put them in some sort of order. I wish I'd had counselling or attended a self-help group at a much younger age. If I had done I think it would have prevented me getting involved with someone so like my father.

'I didn't know about Alateen, though, and I thought counselling was only for older people, so I didn't start it until I was twenty-five. I also wish I'd confided in my mother more as she wasn't in denial about Dad's drinking. Now that I'm a mother I don't want my daughter to go through what I went through and, fortunately, my current partner couldn't be less like my father. He likes a drink but knows when to stop and he treats me with the love and affection I deserve.'

Coming Out

It's only when adult children have accepted the influence of the past that they are ready to deal with the core issues that have been causing them problems as adults, so in some ways the essential starting point is for them to make a conscious decision to 'come out' in a similar way to that by which gays and lesbians decide to end denial about their sexuality. Developing an awareness of those personality traits that need to be corrected can then enable them to be addressed in conjunction with a therapist.

'The initial step in overcoming any bad habit is becoming aware of it. If you have been lying automatically, you are not necessarily aware of what you have been doing. Promise yourself that you will not lie for one whole day. Then see what happens. You may or may not be able to do it.'

Janet Geringer Woititz from *Adult Children of Alcoholics*

A good therapist will try and address the gaps in your development and growth which have been causing problems. They may, for example, emphasize the need to express feelings by encouraging you to cry or advising you to draw up a list of things you feel you are entitled to, such as 'me time' or the right to express your own opinions.

As when dealing with other forms of co-dependency, there is always likely to be a certain amount of trial and error in selecting a suitable therapist, so it is probably worth the adult child identifying a selection of potential options in their locality and cutting their losses early if the sessions aren't working. You are under no obligation to see a course of counselling through to the end, although you are obviously required to pay for any sessions that have already taken place.

Dr Catherine Gilvarry, Programme Convenor of Psychology and Health at Roehampton University, feels there may be limited benefit in seeking out a counsellor who deals exclusively with adult children of alcoholics, but that a good cognitive behavioural therapist (CBT) may be able to help you reformulate your life via regular weekly sessions over three or four months. She points out that no one gets 100 per cent perfect parenting and that children of problem drinkers can benefit from the same therapy that other people seeking to be treated for issues in childhood benefit from.

'Many people have had experiences that are very upsetting,' she explains, 'so adult children are not alone in having experienced profound trauma. There are as many different personality profiles in adult children of problem drinkers as there are in any other group of people, so it's hard to generalize. The reason old unhealthy patterns are perpetuated is that the adult children haven't learned effective coping strategies, so they don't deal in a coherent way with the problems they encounter.'

Gilvarry points out that, for many, the world they grew up in involved neglect and abuse, leaving them with the belief that they are more worthless than those from 'normal' backgrounds; this can make them feel like outsiders in a healthy world. A good CBT therapist can take them through step by step and dismantle their painful conceptions about themselves and the world, focusing on short-term effective treatment rather than replaying old traumas in an unstructured manner.

'CBT gets people to realize that what they believe about and how they think about their problems is at the core of their difficulty,' she explains, 'and it helps people to restructure these thoughts and beliefs in a way that is more productive and healthy for them.'

'Although the suffering manifests itself behaviourally in different ways, children of alcoholics seem to have in common a low self-esteem. This is not surprising, since literature indicates that the conditions which lead an individual to value himself and regard himself as a person of worth can be briefly summarized by the terms "Parental warmth", "clearly defined limits" and "respectful treatment".'

Janet Geringer Woititz from *Adult Children of Alcoholics*

▓ CASE STUDY Talking Provides a Release

It was only when forty-one-year-old Fiona started working as a volunteer for the National Association for Children of Alcoholics (NACOA) in February 2010 that she began to realize her own father's drink problem had in fact had a significant impact on her behaviour.

'When I looked at some of their Powerpoint presentations I realized that I had something missing,' she explains. 'I recognized myself as the adult child of an alcoholic who had hidden their problems by excelling. I had gone full tilt into things to take my mind off it all, and had become very sociable and quite competitive. I excelled both academically and at team sports and had developed very high expectations, and I became very disappointed if I didn't live up to them.

'I have also always found it hard to stick at things. My husband has been in the same job in the police force for twenty-four years, but I have found it difficult to sustain my interest in anything for more than a few years, even though I've had some fantastic jobs. I never found I was able to persevere with them and I always thought I needed to move on.'

Two years ago Fiona returned to working as a commercial model, a career she had originally embarked upon at the age of seventeen. Despite realizing how lucky she was at the time to be doing the type of job most people can only dream about, at the age of twenty-one she switched to being a flight attendant. Between the ages of twenty-six and thirty-nine she proceeded to undertake a variety of sales and marketing roles.

Fiona, who lives in Warwickshire and has two children aged eight and ten, lost her father to cirrhosis of the liver twenty-four years ago when he was aged only fifty-six. Although he had gone dry several times following spells in rehab clinics, he was always back on the whisky again within a few weeks, and during his final years he was knocking back around three bottles a day. Having a job as a publican didn't exactly help his quest for sobriety!

> 'Because the person who should have looked after me wasted their life it has made me determined not to waste mine.'

'He couldn't switch to another line of work as our family money and home was tied up with the business,' explains Fiona. 'So Mum had to take over all the work and he just drank, both in the pub and in our quarters upstairs. He wasn't a nasty drunk and he was always the life and soul of the party, so customers continually bought him drinks. I don't know how my mum managed to stay with him right up until the end, but whenever I asked her why they didn't split up she just used to say it was because she loved him.'

Fiona's father's drinking was rarely ever discussed with either her mother or her older sister. Indeed, neither parent even acknowledged that there was a problem until Fiona was fourteen, when her mother explained that 'having to work because of Daddy's drinking' was the reason why she wasn't able to attend things like school sports days. Indeed, Fiona never discussed the situation with anyone outside the family, not even with her best friend.

'I thought that living with someone like my father was normal life until I started going to other people's houses,' she recalls. 'When I did bring friends home it was a total and utter embarrassment and they were too polite to mention anything, so I brought as few friends home as possible and went to their houses instead.

'A few years ago, when my children started getting to the sort of age at which I had my earliest childhood memories, the very thought of them having to experience the childhood I'd had to endure was heartbreaking. Seeing my husband acting as a father figure to my children and seeing his father be such a fantastic granddad made me realize what I'd been missing and what my children were missing by not having another granddad.'

'Talking about the whole thing has been a real release, and in some ways it's probably similar to someone who is gay taking the decision to come out.'

It was only as a result of experiencing these feelings three years ago that Fiona finally started opening up to her husband and friends about her father, and it wasn't until she started helping out at NACOA this February that she found herself able to have honest conversations with her sister and mother on the subject.

'Talking about the whole thing has been a real release, and in some ways it's probably similar to someone who is gay taking the decision to come out. I used to lie to hide the fact that Dad had died of cirrhosis, and it's all a question of getting over the initial embarrassment of telling people. My mum is now so much happier that she's got someone to talk to on the subject, and a few months ago she admitted for the first time that it was a relief when Dad died. I have even recently discovered that a long-standing friend also had an alcoholic father who died. She had never discussed the subject with anyone, either, but now she talks to me about it all the time.

'NACOA has shown me that there are many other people out there like myself, and a lot of the adult children of alcoholics I talk to when I'm manning the helpline like hearing that it wasn't their fault that their mother or father drank. They often say that perhaps their parent wouldn't have drunk if they hadn't done this or had done that, and they find it very reassuring when I explain that the drinking had nothing to do with their actions.

'I also try to encourage them to be positive and use their experiences to motivate themselves to achieve things, and I'm always emphasizing the importance of having a good sense of humour. Because the person who should have looked after me wasted their life it has made me determined not to waste mine, and I feel that it's important to try and see the funny side of things. If you couldn't laugh you would just give up and cry.'

In summary

- Any child from a problem drinker's household will be adversely affected, and if problems are not addressed they are likely to resurface during adulthood.

- Adult children are more likely than average to develop a drink problem or marry someone with one

- Alateen and confidential specialist national helplines can be very helpful to youngsters and Al-Anon and Adult Children of Alcoholics meetings can benefit adult children, as can finding a suitable therapist

Some Final Words from the Authors

We hope that we have effectively communicated the steps you need to take to survive life with an addict, and that we've given you some ideas that can be tried to help the problem drinker in your life. In particular, the fact that there are now some exciting new treatments available should give all of us who have walked this journey, and are still walking it, a greater sense of optimism that in time much more will be understood about addiction and how it can be treated.

It is our hope and intention that this book will help persuade medical establishments, governments and policy makers worldwide to invest more in understanding the causes and effects of alcohol abuse, to ensure that those approaches that have been demonstrating remarkable potential are given the support and funding they need.

With regard to the more traditional methods and approaches, we appreciate that you may already be familiar with much of what we have referred to, but hopefully we have conveyed some of the main messages in a more coherent format to that in which they have previously been presented. We would also point out that being aware of something doesn't necessarily mean that you are putting it into practice, so you can never have too many reminders.

Even though we have now written two books about alcohol addiction and feel we have tried our hardest to help a number of problem drinkers in our lives, we are the first to acknowledge that we have sometimes fallen short when it comes to looking after our own wellbeing and happiness. We could have done more in the way of attending self-help groups and practising the art of detachment, and we are constantly striving to improve in these respects.

Even if the drinker you have been co-dependent with has died, the healing process is still likely to be ongoing. Furthermore, who can say that you will not find yourself having to cope with another's drink problem in the future? Even if you never have to, you will benefit from applying the art of detachment to others in your life, not just drinkers.

Finally, if we have helped you in any way we would love to hear from you. We can be contacted by email via the book's supporting website on www.beatthebooze.com

Appendix 1

Contact Information

Adult Children of Alcoholics
Worldwide service – www.adultchildren.org

Al-Anon/Alateen
For Al-Anon General Service Office in London providing English meeting information for all of Europe, Asia and Africa (with the exception of South Africa) including the UK visit http://www.al-anon.alateen.org/meetings/unitedkingdom.html. For the US, Canada and countries that do not have a national office of their own visit www.al-anon.alateen.org.

Alcoholics Anonymous (AA)
UK – www.alcoholics-anonymous.org.uk
Worldwide – www.aa.org

Association of Intervention Specialists
For further information on Family Intervention visit
www.associationofinterventionspecialists.org

ClearLife Clinic
www.clearlife.com

Co-Dependents Anonymous (CoDA)
UK – www.coda-uk.org
US – www.coda.org

Dryoutnow.com (For further information on FRAMES)
Tel: 0845 460 1111 or www.dryoutnow.com

Getting Them Sober
www.gettingthemsober.com

Lookatyourdrinking.com
www.lookatyourdrinking.com

Moderation Management
www.moderation.org

National Association for Children of Alcoholics (NACOA)
UK helpline – 0800 358 3456
UK website – visit www.nacoa.org.uk

Neurofeedback
www.eeginfo.com

SMART Recovery
Worldwide – www.smartrecovery.org

SOS International
Worldwide – www.sossobriety.org

5-Step Method
www.alcoholdrugsandfamilies.nhs.uk

Appendix 2

Further Reading, Sources and Copyright

Every effort has been made to contact the copyright holders of material reproduced in this book. If any have been inadvertently overlooked, the publishers will be pleased to make restitution at the earliest opportunity.

Adult Children of Alcoholics, Janet Geringer Woititz (Health Communications, 1983)

Alcohol and Drug Misuse, G. Hussein Rassool (Routledge, 2009). Excerpt quoted is from p.82

Alcoholism: The Cause & the Cure, Genita Petralli (Alternative Approaches to end Alcohol Abuse, 1999)

'Behavioural Couples Therapy for Alcoholism and Drug Abuse, a Guideline Developed For the Behavioural Health Recovery Management Project', Timothy J. O'Farrell and William Fals-Stewart

'Behavioural Couples Therapy (BCT) For Alcohol and Drug Use Disorders: a Meta-analysis', M.B. Powers, E. Vedel and P.M.G. Emmelkamp (*Clinical Psychology Review*, 2008, 28 (6) pp.952–962

Changing Course: Healing from Loss, Abandonment, and Fear, Claudia Black PhD (Hazelden, 2002)

Co-dependent No More: How to Stop Controlling Others and Start Caring for Yourself, Melody Beattie (Hazelden, 1986)

Controlling Your Drinking, William R. Miller PhD and Ricardo F. Muñoz PhD (The Guilford Press, 2005)

Courage To Be Me: Living With Alcoholism (Al-Anon Family Group Headquarters, Inc., 1996). Reprinted by permission of Al-Anon Family Group Headquarters, Inc. Permission to reprint this excerpt does not mean that Al-Anon Family Group Headquarters, Inc. has reviewed or approved the contents of this publication, or that Al-Anon Family Group Headquarters, Inc. necessarily agrees with the views expressed herein. Al-Anon is a programme of recovery for families and friends of alcoholics and use of this excerpt in any non Al-Anon context does not imply endorsement or affiliation by Al-Anon

Detachment: the Art of Letting Go While Living With an Alcoholic, Evelyn Leite (Hazelden, 1988)

Don't Let the Bastards Grind You Down, Georgia W. (Ornery Tiger Press, 2008)

The Easy Way to Control Alcohol, Allen Carr (Arcturus Publishing, 2009)

From Survival to Recovery (Al-Anon Family Group Headquarters, Inc. 2007) Reprinted by permission of Al-Anon Family Group Headquarters, Inc. Permission to reprint this excerpt does not mean that Al-Anon Family Group Headquarters, Inc. has reviewed or approved the contents of this publication, or that Al-Anon Family Group Headquarters, Inc. necessarily agrees with the views expressed herein. Al-Anon is a programme of recovery for families and friends of alcoholics and use of this excerpt in any non Al-Anon context does not imply endorsement or affiliation by Al-Anon

Games Alcoholics Play, Claude Steiner PhD (Ballantine Books, 1971)

Getting Them Sober, Volume 2, Toby Rice Drews (Recovery Communications Inc., 1983) See www.gettingthemsober.com

Get Your Loved One Sober, Robert J. Meyers PhD and Brenda L. Wolfe PhD (Hazelden, 2004)

If You Loved Me, You'd Stop!, Lisa Frederiksen (KLJ Publishing, 2008)

It Will Never Happen to Me!, Claudia Black (Ballantine Books, 1981)

Love First: a Family Guide to Intervention (2nd Edition), Jeff Jay and Debra Jay (Hazelden, 2008)

Marriage on the Rocks, Janet Geringer Woititz (Health Communications Inc., 1979)

No More Hangovers, Allen Carr (Arcturus Publishing, 2010)

Perfect Daughters, Robert J. Ackerman (Health Communications Inc., 2002)

Recovery: A Guide for Adult Children of Alcoholics, Herbert L. Gravitz and Julie D. Bowden (Fireside, 1987).

'The 5-Step Method: a research-based programme of work to help family members affected by a relative's alcohol or drug misuse'. Drugs: Education, Prevention and Policy, 17 (S1), The Alcohol, Drugs and the Family Research Group: Alex Copello, Akanidomo Ibanga, Jim Orford, Lorna Templeton and Richard Velleman (2010)

The Courage to Change, Dennis Wholey (Grand Central Publishing, 1994)

The Cure For Alcoholism, Roy Eskapa (BenBella Books, 2008)

The Easy Way to Stop Drinking, Allen Carr (Sterling Publishing, 2005). Excerpt from p.139.

The End of My Addiction, Dr Olivier Ameisen (Piatkus Books, 2009). Excerpts from *Heal Thyself*, Olivier Ameisen 2009, 2010. Originally published under the title, *The End of My Addiction*. Reprinted by permission of Farrar, Strauss and Giroux, LLC

The Language of Letting Go, Melody Beattie (Hazelden, 1990)

Under the Influence, James R. Milam PhD and Katherine Ketcham (Bantam Books, 1983)

7 Weeks to Safe Social Drinking, Donna J. Cornett (People Friendly Books, 2005)

Index